How we fell in love with

ITALIAN FOOD

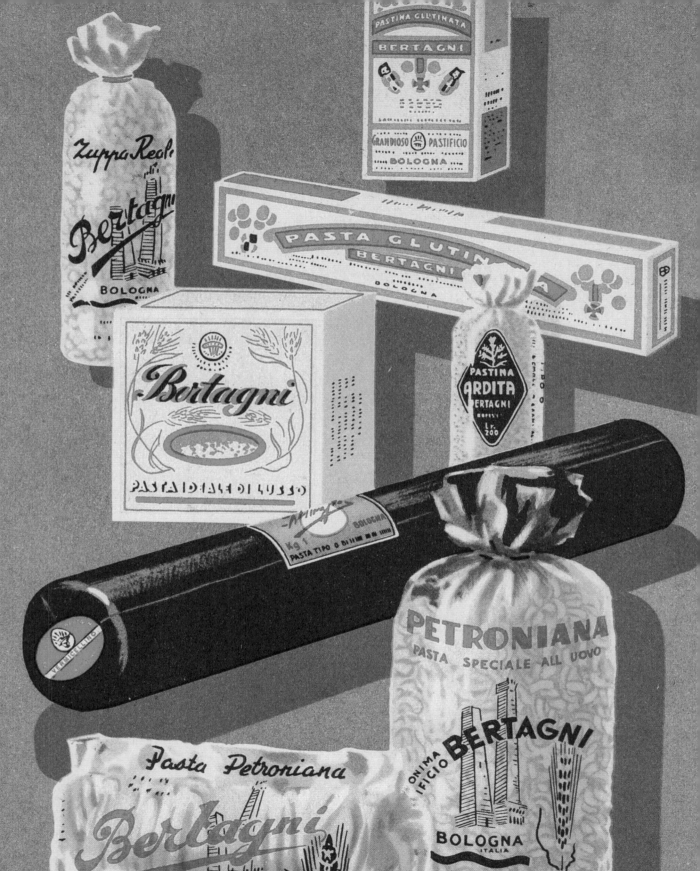

How we fell in love with
ITALIAN FOOD

Diego Zancani

Bodleian Library
UNIVERSITY OF OXFORD

CONTENTS

ACKNOWLEDGEMENTS

FIRST AND FOREMOST I wish to thank Valentina Olivastri, who has helped me
all the way in researching and preparing this book. It is as much hers as mine.
I am particularly grateful to Anna Masetti, Sue Osborne and Sebastian Peattie for
their patient reading of the whole manuscript. Invaluable remarks, suggestions
and materials were provided also by Anna Bensted, Roberto Bruni, Paul Howard,
Lino Pertile, Massimo Spigaroli and Joseph Trivelli, and by Leo, Sandro and Fabio
Zancani. I am grateful to the editorial team of Bodleian Library Publishing, in
particular to Samuel Fanous, Janet Phillips and Leanda Shrimpton, and to the staff
of the Bodleian Libraries in Oxford, especially to Julie Anne Lambert, Librarian
of the John Johnson Collection, and the anonymous reader for providing useful
comments and advice. Penny Padovani of Padovani Books kindly offered to put
me in touch with Enzo Apicella concerning the use of a few of his drawings, for
which I am particularly grateful. A big thank you to Gioia Olivastri for providing
some of the photographs and to Dr Peter and Caroline Cannon-Brookes for
allowing me access to their vast collection of art illustrations. And finally, special
thanks to the able providers of rare recipes and sustenance during research trips:
Lella Zancani and Maria Grazia Zancani.

1. HOW IT ALL STARTED

I HAD MY FIRST TASTE OF BRITISH FOOD when I moved to the UK in the late 1960s. The University of Reading, where I was teaching at the time, put me up with a local family who, day in day out, would feed me the classic meat and two veg – some carrots and a handful of peas boiled in unsalted water, all dished up with no condiments whatsoever. The peas were particularly sad, and when I asked for a drop of olive oil – I did not think it an unreasonable request but little did I know – Mrs Porter gave me a suspicious look, and suggested I should call in at the chemist's. When I did so, the girl behind the counter at Boots handed me a tiny bottle filled with what looked like an oily substance and told me to put a few drops in my ears before bedtime. Contrary to instructions, I added it to my veg, and the landlady's little daughter, after asking what it was, shouted 'Yuk!'[1]

True, the 'olive oil' turned out to be utterly tasteless but, given the circumstance, it was better than nothing. And while I was slowly working my way through the peas, I wondered what had happened to the tradition of imports established by the Romans two thousand years ago. At that time, and for a few centuries after, regular shipments of olives and olive oil were delivered to Southampton and English ports in the Thames estuary. After all, as everyone knows from *Monty Python*, the Romans introduced a few good things to their colonies, including sanitation, education and the creation of aqueducts. They also imported wine and brought peace – and peas too, for that matter – as well as many more vegetables and herbs such as rosemary, thyme, bay, basil and mint.

Before the arrival of the Romans, it appears that even wild ingredients growing in Iron Age Britain were in short supply. As for fruit, only crab apples were available together with a few berries, such as raspberries, bilberries, blackberries and elderberries. According to Julius Caesar's account of his campaigns, Britons lived on milk and meat alone, but they were quite choosy. Some did not eat hares, hens and geese, because they were believed to bring bad luck.[2] However, they did not mind rearing them for their fur, eggs and feathers.

There is evidence, however, that long before the Roman invasion, members of the Celtic elite in the south of England were carrying on trade with Roman Gaul. Some of them, interested in more exotic provisions, must have seemed like early gastro-snobs who preferred to go beyond the ordinary diet. They were trading some grains and precious metals in exchange for olives, wine, fish sauce and probably some olive oil, judging from the amphorae that have been found near the Thames.[3]

FEEDING THE ROMAN ARMY

Roman soldiers needed wheat for their daily bread. By this time, bread appears to have superseded the old cereal and pulse pottages, or thick soups, of ancient Rome and was now a staple of the soldiers' diet. Sometimes wheat had to be gathered on the spot and some military units were equipped with a sickle, so that they could reap their own grain in other people's fields.

Once the occupation force was well established, the Romans started cultivating gardens and orchards in which fruit trees, such as apples (domestic apples, that is), pears, cherries, plums and damsons, were planted.[4] Pliny the Elder, one of the greatest naturalists of antiquity, went as far as dating the moment when the cherry, which had been thriving in Rome for about two hundred years, 'crossed the ocean and got as far as Britain'. He stated that cherries were originally imported to Rome from the Black Sea by General Lucius Lucullus after 74 BCE and 120 years later they reached Britain. Pliny also expounds on the great variety of cherries available, but does not tell us which one reached Britain first.[5]

and produced in numerous towns along the shores of the Mediterranean and later even in Britain. If we were to advertise it today, it would be marketed as a dipping sauce just like Thai fish sauce or Vietnamese *nuoc mam cham*.

Garum, which is also often mentioned in Roman culinary literature, used to be considered an equivalent term to *liquamen*, but is now believed to have been different. Originally made by the Greeks, who used a fish called *garos*, it was fermented mainly with blood from mackerel and other fish, and

Fragment of a Roman fresco panel, showing the preparation of venison

would have been reliant on a specific pollinating agent, the tiny caprificatory wasp, and this did not exist in Roman Britain.)

The Romans loved adopting domestic customs, and incorporating local deities when necessary in their religious ceremonies, but as far as food was concerned they certainly had a preference for a Mediterranean diet, with cereals and a variety of vegetables, as well as meat. Bones from a variety of animals have been found in most archaeological sites dating from this period. The top brass of the Roman army did not share the native population's fondness for sheep, and preferred pork, although lambs were used in sacrificial ceremonies, and so consumed that way.

The Romans were keen on improving livestock breeding, and domestic pigs, along with some larger types of cattle, became more common. Pork products were definitely favourite foods. Hams, sausages, pork cutlets, lard and pig's trotters are all mentioned in some of the most fascinating records that have survived: they come from the rubbish of a military garrison in the north of England, near Hadrian's Wall, called Vindolanda. Despite being a remote posting in the far northern reaches of the Roman empire, Vindolanda was not just a billet of rough-living soldiers; their wives and families were there too – excavations at Vindolanda have uncovered, among much else, the remains of small leather children's shoes.[13] Among the lists of provisions and requests for leave of absence found on the site are other documents of a more personal nature. From fragments of letters we know, for example, that Sulpicia Lepidina, the wife of a military chief, Praefectus Flavius Cerialis, was invited by her friend Claudia Severa to a birthday party.[14] We can only guess what was served in terms of food, but in one account some *turtas* are mentioned. These were probably a kind of twisted bread, made with milk and garnished with a sprinkle of poppy seeds on top.[15] The only cookery book surviving from those times is a compilation of recipes attributed to Apicius, the most renowned gourmet of antiquity, but actually written by various practising cooks and produced much later, probably in the fourth century. In this collection there is no mention of *turtas* per se, but various sweet dishes do feature, including the following pear concoction:

PATINA DE PIRIS
Core and boil the pears, pound them with pepper, cumin, honey *passum* [a raisin wine], *liquamen*, and a little oil. Add eggs to make a *patina* [plate, dish], sprinkle with pepper and serve.
Apicius 4, 2.35.

Sally Grainger, one of the editors of the most recent critical edition of *Apicius*, considers an adaptation of this as one of the most popular dishes in her dinner parties (see Pear Patina, overleaf). A particularly refreshing summer salad made with melon and mint from *Apicius* 3.7 could also be mentioned. Grainger recommends it as an alternative to sorbet at a modern dinner party between courses, as well as a potential dessert (see Melon with Mint Dressing, p. 19).

PEAR PATINA

700g (1 ½ lb) Conference pears
200ml (7 fl oz) red wine
50ml (2 fl oz or 3 tbsp) *passum* (raisin wine)
2 tbsp clear honey
1 tbsp olive oil
1–2 tbsp fish sauce
4 eggs
1 tsp cumin
generous freshly ground black pepper

Peel and core the pears and chop them roughly. Cook them till soft in the wine and *passum*. Pass the whole mixture through a sieve or process it until smooth. Add the honey, olive oil, fish sauce and 4 eggs, and beat smooth again. Dry-roast the cumin and grind to a fine powder. Add it to the custard, then season with black pepper. Pour into a greased casserole dish and bake for 20 minutes, or until it sets, in a moderate oven (375°F, 190°C, mark 5). Serve warm with a final sprinkling of freshly ground black pepper.[16]

MELON WITH MINT DRESSING

1 round sweet ripe melon such as Galia, honeydew, etc.
generous freshly ground black pepper
2 tsp dried mint or 3 tsp fresh chopped pennyroyal or
culinary mint
2 dessert spoons runny honey
1 dessert spoon fish sauce
2 dessert spoons wine vinegar

Cut the melon into quarters and take the flesh off the skin. Dice the flesh and place in the serving dish. Combine the other ingredients and whisk until the honey is fully combined. Pour over the melon about 15 minutes before it is to be served and turn the fruit over in the sauce. Chill and serve with cocktail sticks to pick the pieces up.[17]

Roman Britain lasted nearly four hundred years. Traditionally 410 CE is the year in which the Roman occupation ended, and a period of chaos ensued with raids carried out by Germanic tribes, and much uncertainty. However, there were new types of trading settlements on navigable rivers in Anglo-Saxon times, from the end of the sixth century to the beginning of the eighth. Saxon merchants also attended the important annual fair of St Denis in Paris from 634 BCE onwards, and it is likely that some importing of olive oil and wine continued as in Roman times, with the addition of fruit, nuts and hops.[18] In the eighth and ninth centuries clergymen from Britain embarked on annual expeditions to Rome 'to confer with the Pope' and presumably carried out some trade. The details of the return journey from Rome by Archbishop Sigeric of Canterbury in 993 have come down to us.[19] It was a journey of about twelve weeks, and although the purpose was to visit most of the important churches along the way, it is likely that his party indulged in some exchanges of goods with the local populations. We also know that in the eighth century London was already considered a great 'emporium for many nations who come to it by land and sea'.[20] In other words it was an important trading place, where all sorts of produce could be found. Some information on the importance of banquets in Anglo-Saxon times can be gathered from literary and historical sources, such as *Beowulf*, and early Latin chronicles. Food was a powerful marker of the social status of the eater, and individuals who enjoyed large chunks of meat were recognized as having potential as leaders. There is reason to believe that the spreading of Christianity brought, as well as monasteries, some 'continental' practices to England, such as eating more bread and vegetables, in addition to an interest in restricted diets, including the eating of fish on certain days.[21]

THE NORMAN CONQUEST

Huge changes occurred after 1066, when Duke William II of Normandy claimed the throne of England, not least to the language of food. While the aristocracy used Norman French, the lower classes spoke Anglo-Saxon, and the differences reflected in their respective vocabularies are still with us today.

To take just one example: the different terms for meat. The Anglo-Saxon *pig*, once cooked or cured, becomes gentrified as *pork*, from a Norman word derived from Latin. *Sheep* is also an Anglo-Saxon word, but the French *mouton* for the same animal has become *mutton* in modern English; similarly, the meat of the Anglo-Saxon *ox* became *beef*, from the French *boeuf* (derived from the Latin *bovem*). All this is significant not only for food and for the contacts between different cultures, but for social history as well. The linguistic difference highlights the distance between the workers who looked after the farm animals, and the higher classes who enjoyed the produce.

Although it is tempting to think of England in the Middle Ages as cut off from the rest of Europe and developing in its own way, without undue influence from other nations, this is actually untrue.[22] The Conquest created strong ties between England and the Continent, and one of the culinary developments that reflected Norman influence was the increased use of spices. They were still carried overland, following the routes established in Roman times, and by sea, especially on Venetian and Genoese vessels.[23] Venetian galleys continued their trade to London and Southampton until the middle of the sixteenth century. The arrival of Eleanor of Aquitaine in 1152, following her marriage to Henry II, may also have contributed to the English adoption of new and intriguing oriental spices that she would have come across when campaigning in the Holy Land with her first husband, Louis VII of France.

Spices that had been popular in Roman times, such as *laser* or *laserpicium*, a resin producing a type of asafoetida, and *silphium*, were being supplanted in the Middle Ages by cinnamon, cloves and nutmeg, together with ginger and saffron. Pepper remained quite popular, its use not diminishing until the eighteenth century (when it became 'too common', and therefore shunned by the higher classes). Interest in aromatics never waned through the Middle Ages. Pepper, cloves and cinnamon were added to most dishes, and possibly nutmeg too, although this and mace may have been purchased primarily for the medicine cupboard rather than the kitchen.[24] The idea, however, that spices were added to dishes to cover the taste of decayed meat is completely inaccurate, and now generally discounted. Meat was consumed fresh fairly soon after slaughtering, or preserved by smoking or salting. Spices were used medicinally because they were thought to balance the properties of certain foods. Also, they were rare and expensive, and therefore considered a status symbol.

It is possible that the translations of Arab treatises on early medicine may have influenced medieval doctors in various parts of Europe, though it is unlikely that the use of spices in Italy or in Britain was directly due to the Arabs themselves.[25] There is, however, evidence that recipes from twelfth-century Norman collections were indebted to Arabic sources. This would have been mainly through the contacts of Muslim cooks at the court of the Norman kings of Sicily, especially William II, whose wife was the daughter of England's Henry II.[26]

In collections of English recipes from the late fourteenth century, we find mention of numerous herbs, including borage, chervil, spring onions, clary sage and dittany (a type of oregano), and even more spices: caraway, canel (cinnamon), cloves, cumin, galingale, 'grains de parys' (grains of paradise or *melegueta*, a type of precious pepper), long pepper, pistachio nuts (called *festicade*) and mustard. One recipe for 'Lombard mustard' consisted of ground mustard seeds previously dried in an oven, well crushed in a mortar with the addition of some honey, wine and vinegar.[27]

A few foodstuffs that we take for granted today were, in the England of the Middle Ages, exotic and treated as spices. Sugar was one of these (honey was the main sweetener of dishes), and rice was another.[28] Rice was imported by the Arabs into Sicily in the twelfth century and then to Spain, and over the next couple of centuries its use spread northwards; by the fifteenth century the dukes of Milan were fostering its cultivation in the Lombard marshes. The medieval recipe for 'Lombard rice', an ancestor of modern risotto, contains spices – ginger, clove and mace, and saffron was also popular – as well as the yolks of hard-boiled eggs.

When rice reached English houses, it was ground and locked up as a precious item together with the other spices. Medieval expenditure accounts provide a wealth of fascinating information. The household accounts of Dame Alice de Bryene, for example, showed only three pounds of rice consumed during 1418–19, but in the previous century, the Countess of Leicester used

110lb (50kg) in just four months between Christmas and April 1265.[29] Maybe she was very keen on blancmange, made at this time with rice, almond milk and white meat or fish pounded to a smooth paste, with the addition of fat and sugar.

THE ARRIVAL OF PASTA

The legend that noodles were brought to Italy by Marco Polo (1254–1324) is utterly spurious. The story was probably invented by the Macaroni National Manufacturers Association of America, and appeared in the late 1920s in their publication *The Macaroni Journal*.[30]

The first forms of pasta probably arrived in Italy when the Arabs introduced a form of thin dried noodles, called *itriyya*.[31] We know from Muhammad al-Idrisi, the Moroccan-born geographer of Roger II, Norman king of Sicily, of a factory for dried pasta near Palermo in Sicily, which exported it to most of the Mediterranean. And a basket, or barrel, full of 'macaroni' is mentioned in the inventory of the possessions of a soldier from Genoa as early as 1279, which confirms the importance of that area for dried pasta.

Lasagne and gnocchi were often mentioned in poems and tales from the end of the thirteenth century onwards.[32] In a humorous ballad recorded in a document of *c*.1282 in Bologna, two women textile workers go out on a drinking spree to a local inn, where they also manage to eat huge portions (seven plates) of gnocchi and lasagne. The great fourteenth-century storyteller Giovanni Boccaccio featured many pasta dishes in his *Decameron*, including macaroni and ravioli with butter and grated Parmesan.

The road of pasta towards global success was still far in the future, but by the fourteenth century the long journey of Italian pasta was truly under way, and England was one of the first places to adopt it.

One of the best known poets in the whole of English literature, Geoffrey Chaucer (*c*.1343–1400), the son of a wealthy vintner, was sent on several occasions to Italy for diplomatic and trading negotiations. At least three trips are on record, and it seems impossible that a writer who showed an

ꝛ li bien se pꝛouuoit / ꝛ eltoit li cremus
Q ua senseigue poꝛter / su soꝛ tous esleus
ꝛ aymes len kierka / qui niert mie espous
ꝛ ant itrencha de hyaumes / tant ipcha desca

Cooks working in a medieval kitchen, depicted on the margin of a fifteenth-century manuscript

interest in the food available in London, and who included a cook among his travellers (many of whom were quite keen on the pleasures of the table) in *The Canterbury Tales*, was uninterested in Italian food.[33] Unfortunately no letters or diary can support this claim, but we can speculate that when Chaucer was sent to Genoa in 1372–73 to meet the Doge on behalf of the king of England to discuss the use of an English port by Genoese ships, he was offered some local specialities. At least two possible candidates spring to mind, given Genoa's fame as a centre for the production of dried pasta. Both are mentioned in thirteenth- and early fourteenth-century Italian manuscripts: lasagne and a kind of macaroni. Moreover we know that in 1351 some 'master lasagne workers' were hired by a Genoese merchant ship, and therefore it is fair to assume that this type of pasta was popular and consumed by the crew.[34]

A recipe for lasagne from this era is remarkably simple. White flour is mixed with lukewarm water, and thin sheets of the resulting dough or paste (pasta) are produced and left to dry. They are then boiled in a good broth,

E n fin quant repairier / vaut a son herbergage
l e boin duc enmena / si fu de son manage
A rchade li donna / quil tenoit sans seruage
z li dus le serui / sans vilte z sans outrage

preferably made with capon or other fatty meat, and served layered with some
good grated cheese in each layer. In the same recipe collection another dish
is specifically indicated as 'Genoese'. This is another type of thin pasta, called
tria (recalling the Arabic *itriyya*), cooked in almond milk, and mainly used for
convalescents.

I am not, of course, claiming that Chaucer brought back the recipes,
but in the oldest English cookery manuscripts, of the fourteenth century,
collectively known as the *Curye on Inglysch*, we find some dishes that may have
been inspired by Italy.[35]

The first one is called *losyns* (or *loseyns*) and it probably refers to the type
of pasta shaped as a lozenge, but the procedure is the familiar one of lasagne.
And the recipe is virtually identical to that found in a fourteenth-century
Italian *Libro della cucina*.[36] Typically, the strips of pasta were dried, boiled,
plated in three or four layers and served with grated cheese and some sweet
spices, mainly cinnamon.[37] This addition of sweet spices might seem a little

odd, but while staying with family and friends in Tuscany I decided to experiment with it. I used a form of wide, thick tagliatelle, and tossed the pasta with butter, grated Parmesan, a little cinnamon powder and one ground clove. Although my guests were a little suspicious at first, my gamble paid off, and they all licked their forks clean: Renaissance-style tagliatelle went down a treat and kept those around my table very happy. The mixture of sweet and savoury worked perfectly well and the butter fried on a low heat until it became the colour of hazelnuts made it wonderfully smooth.

MEDIEVAL RECIPES

No recipes, however scantily described, have survived either from the Anglo-Saxon period, or from that of the early English kingdoms. But people did travel between Britain and the Italian peninsula – Giraldus Cambrensis (Gerald of Wales, *c*.1146–1223), for example, visited Rome three times, in 1199, 1201 and 1203 – and they presumably reported some details about daily life and food in Italy.

It is difficult to establish links between culinary traditions in distant countries 700 or so years ago, but there were numerous opportunities for exchanges of practical information concerning crafts and trades, and food would have been a part of this. From the thirteenth century onwards Italian merchants and bankers, especially from Lombardy and Tuscany, established trade contacts in the south of England to buy the excellent wool produced there. Lombard Street in London is a reminder of their settlement, and the cachet connected with this region has remained to characterize a number of dishes.[38] Among the recipes collected in the *Curye on Inglysch*, apart from 'Lombard rice' and 'Lumbard mustard', we also find *leche lumbard*, a spiced boiled pudding of pork, raisins, dates and eggs in a sauce of wine and almond milk, with powdered cinnamon and ginger.

Platina (Bartolomeo Sacchi), the author of an innovative book on cooking and health, pays homage to Pope Sixtus IV, fresco, c.1477, by Melozzo da Forli (1438–94)

TEMPLA DOMVM EXPOSITIS·VICOS FORA MOENIA PONTES·
VIRGINEAM TRIVII QVOD REPARARIS AQVAM·
PRISCA LICET NAVTIS STATVAS DARE COMMODA PORTVS·
ET VATICANVM CINGERE SIXTE IVGVM·
PLVS TAMEN VRBS DEBET·NAM QVAE SQVALORE LATEBAT·
CERNITVR IN CELEBRI BIBLIOTHECA LOCO

It is only in the fourteenth century that proper collections of recipes start to appear in manuscripts. Some, like *leche lumbard*, have a noticeable 'oriental' influence in the widespread use of almond milk as a basis for sauces, or as a cooking medium. This may have come from Spain or Italy, both influenced by Arab cookery from the eighth to the tenth centuries, because as far as we know almond milk is never mentioned in Roman cookery.[39]

Lasagne is not the only Italian dish to feature in the *Curye on Inglysch*. Here we also find a recipe for *ravioles*, a mixture of grated cheese with butter encased in little parcels made with thin layers of pasta. The *ravioles* would then be boiled in a tasty broth, laid out on a plate and served with melted butter and grated cheese 'beneath and above', and sprinkled with a pinch of ground spices, usually cinnamon and cloves.[40]

Another recipe, which appears immediately after the *ravioles*, is also inspired by an Italian type of pasta, which was to have much success in the following centuries: macaroni. In Italian, as *maccheroni*, the word originally referred to pasta dumplings (gnocchi), and only later, in southern Italy, did it turn into the familiar tubular form. In the medieval English recipe, *Makerouns* look more like vermicelli ('little worms'), which only appeared later in England. The word *maccheroni* was traditionally explained as coming from Greek or Latin *maccare*, meaning to pound or crush. However, it is more likely to have been invented by the Arabs, as the word *maqroun* referred to little rings of pasta, made with durum wheat.[41]

Recipes for meat dumplings often appear in England under the name of *tartlettes*, *turteletes*, or *torteletys*, the last being closest to the Italian original *tortelletti*.[42] These pasta dumplings had different fillings, and in early Italian recipes they were also indicated by colour: white ones were made with a filling of cheese, and green with a filling of spinach and herbs.[43] These, like their Asian equivalents, such as Japanese *gyoza* or their Chinese relatives *jaozi*, could be boiled or fried.

Sometimes pasta dumplings even shed their pasta casings. The following dish is mentioned in a chronicle written by Salimbene de Adam, a Franciscan monk from Parma, *c.*1282. He tells us that one day in August he ate, for the first time, some 'ravioli without any pasta wrapping'. He pretended to

GNUDI

Serves 6–8 (10–12 *gnudi* per person)
1kg (2lb) spinach
300g (10–12 oz) ricotta (ideally made with ewe's milk)
2 eggs
100g (4oz) freshly grated Parmesan
½ tsp grated nutmeg
50g (2oz) white flour
salt and pepper
a few sage leaves

First wash the spinach. To cook it, heat one teaspoon of olive oil in a large pan, add the spinach to the pan and a pinch of salt, cover. No more water should be necessary. In about 3–4 minutes, the spinach should be ready. Remove and put in a colander. When cooled a little, make sure that you remove as much of the moisture as possible by squeezing it with your hands, or by putting a weight over the spinach in the colander. Chop the spinach, and squeeze again if necessary.

In a large bowl, add the spinach to the ricotta passed through a sieve (or possibly, if it is very fresh, left to drain overnight). Add a generous pinch of grated nutmeg, the grated Parmesan, the eggs and some salt and pepper. Mix well. Taste the mixture, and adjust the seasoning.

At this point, using some flour, start making fairly small-sized balls (about 3cm or 1in diameter) in your hands, adding more flour if necessary. Place all the naked ravioli on a tray or a clean cloth and sprinkle with a little flour.

Boil some water in a large pan, add some salt, and then carefully drop the naked ravioli into the water. They will be cooked in less than 5 minutes. Remove them carefully with a slotted spoon and arrange them in a well-greased oven dish, pour over some melted butter, then sprinkle over a few sage leaves and grated Parmesan. Slide under a grill for a few minutes and serve hot. In Tuscany they also serve them with a meat and tomato sauce, rather than grilling.

frown upon them, as something certainly invented by gluttonous people, but obviously enjoyed them.[44] They are still made in Florence, where they are known as *gnudi* or 'the naked ones', but they are also found in central and northern Italy, with various names, such as *malfatti* (the badly shaped ones), or green dumplings. I have recently found *gnudi* on the menu of a central London restaurant.

Open tarts were also popular in the Mediterranean and in England. A tart of cheese curds with egg whites, sugar and elder blooms was described in an English medieval manuscript as *sambocade*.[45] The word comes from the Latin name of the plant, *Sambucus*, and elderflowers were often mentioned in medieval Italian recipes. Bartolomeo Sacchi, known as Platina (1421–1481), a scholar and the author of an innovative treatise on food and good health, mentions the importance of elderflowers, and includes a number of recipes for them in his book, including an elderflower *torte* which has remarkable similarities to the *sambocade*, made with curd, sugar and rosewater.[46] This, like most recipes mentioned by Platina, derives from his friend Master Martino de' Rossi, one of the greatest cooks of early Renaissance Italy, who moved between the courts of cardinals, *condottieri* and other prominent leaders, such as Francesco Sforza, Duke of Milan.[47] There are striking similarities in Martino's work with some English dishes whose ingredients included fresh cheese, plenty of egg whites, sugar and ginger, butter and milk, plus elderflowers.[48]

Did any typically Italian meat dish exist in medieval Britain? Were Britons already fond of *osso buco*? Difficult to say, but in the *Curye on Inglysch* there is an intriguing recipe for *Veel in buknade*, or simply *bukkenade*.[49] This is a veal stew characterized by the small 'mouthfuls' into which the meat was cut, *bocconi* or *bocconata* in Italian. It would be a leap to connect *bukkenade* with *osso buco*, despite the similarity of name, but this well-known veal dish may be an echo of a medieval recipe.

Literature often represents food as something to be desired. In his *Decameron* Boccaccio gives a vivid picture of a most extravagant land of plenty. There, excellent ravioli and macaroni are cooked on top of hills made of Parmesan cheese and covered with vines tied up with sausages. Once ready, the pasta morsels start tumbling down the hill towards a stream of the purest and best Vernaccia wine.[50] Readers of Boccaccio's tales must have found these stories irresistible, so much so that they decided to go and check for themselves. The era of the foodie was about to commence.

OSSO BUCO MILANESE·STYLE

Serves 4

4 slices shin of veal, approx. 2.5cm (1in) thick. *You may have to ask your butcher to cut them, and make sure that each piece has bone marrow in it. You can also use shin of beef, which is much easier to find, but it may be too large, and would take longer to cook.*

2 tbsp plain flour

40g (1½oz) butter

1½ tbsp olive oil

1 onion, chopped

1 stick celery, chopped

1 small carrot, chopped

150ml (5 fl oz) dry red wine, Barbera, Chianti or similar. *(I use red wine because I like stronger flavours and I prefer the colour it produces in the finished dish, but a fruity white wine that is not too acidic, such as Orvieto or Pecorino, is perfectly fine.)*

150ml (5 fl oz) beef, veal or chicken stock; a cube may be used instead

salt and pepper

For the *gremolata*

3 tbsp finely chopped flat leaf parsley

1 small clove garlic, peeled and chopped

zest from 1 lemon

1 tsp orange zest (optional)

Sprinkle the shin of veal with the flour. Heat the butter and oil on medium heat and brown the meat for about 3–4 minutes on each side. Add the onion, celery and carrot, and fry gently for about 10 minutes. Pour the wine in the pan and let it simmer for a couple of minutes, lower the heat, and stir. Cover the pan and simmer for about 1½ hours, or up to 2 hours, stirring occasionally and making sure that the sauce is not becoming too dry. If so, just add a tablespoon or two of meat stock. At this point the meat should be very tender.

Prepare the *gremolata* by chopping the parsley with the garlic and adding the lemon zest (plus the orange zest, if you are using), with a little salt and pepper. Sprinkle this mixture over each piece of meat, and taste. Leave it for one minute or so and serve.

Osso buco is usually served with some saffron risotto, but some sautéed spinach and potato purée would do very well. Personally I quite like adding a few peeled tomatoes, just after the wine, but this, like potato purée, would obviously have been impossible in past centuries.

2. EARLY ENGLISH TRAVELLERS TO ITALY

AFTER THE (RE)DISCOVERY OF THE AMERICAS IN 1492, the world seemed to have expanded, but news about novel products and exotic foods was slow to spread. Bright young things from wealthy families were often keen to learn about new customs of foreign lands, and curious to know what existed across the ocean, but the most usual motive for travelling abroad, apart from trade or war, was spiritual.

A long pilgrimage to see relics, and visit churches to obtain special 'discounts' for one's sins, known as indulgences, was considered an excellent investment for the soul. The more relics one saw, the more places connected with early Christians one visited and prayed at, the shorter the period your soul would have to spend in purgatory 'cleansing' itself before ascending to Heaven.[1] Consequently, pilgrims were very willing to undertake long journeys in order to obtain the best of indulgences, but embarking on a long voyage was a tricky affair.

Coaches were rare before the seventeenth century, and although horses were a common means of transport, most people travelled on foot. This was known as 'going around on St Francis' horse', the Italian equivalent of 'Shanks's pony' – Francis being the saint who famously did not even own a donkey. Little was known about foreign lands. Maps were not common, although a few 'guides for pilgrims' were available in print, and legends were rife.[2] A letter of credit and letters of introduction to important people along the way were definitely necessary, together with a series of travel permits. Just journeying the length of the Italian peninsula from north to south meant crossing at least nine or ten independent states.

Travellers often kept diaries, jotting down their impressions on the move or upon their return to England. Some may have had an impact on friends and family who wanted to know more about foreign people's customs and diets. Fortunately for us, many of those personal accounts have survived, including one by our first traveller.

First, and most importantly, she was a woman, the daughter of a wealthy merchant from Lynn (now King's Lynn). Margery Kempe (*c.*1373–after 1438) was a mystic and a visionary, inspired to go on pilgrimage to the Holy Land and to Rome by none other than God himself.[3] Despite being illiterate, Margery was determined to tell her story, which, on returning to England, she first dictated to her son, and later to a priest.

She probably set off from Great Yarmouth in 1413 with a group of fellow pilgrims. She first landed in the Netherlands, crossed Germany and then Switzerland.[4] Her diary makes no mention of cities in northern Italy until she reaches Bologna, which she calls 'the grace'. This had nothing to do with her religious fervour but with the Italian term *la grassa* meaning 'the fat one', implying great richness. This sobriquet started in the Middle Ages because of the abundant food provisions available in the city and the quality of its well-known pork products. (Bologna sausage, much prized at the time, only much later became American boloney sausage, and subsequently *baloney* to mean 'nonsense'.) The other adjective attributed to Bologna was *la dotta*, 'the learned one', because of its ancient university.

Eventually, in the spring of 1414, Margery reached Venice, at the time one of the richest cities in the world. La Serenissima, as the city in the lagoon was known, was expanding its territories into mainland Italy, and probably had a population of over 100,000. Jews and Turks lived and traded side by side with Christians, and merchants from all over the world, including some from the Far East who had followed one of the Silk Roads, added to the cosmopolitan bustle. Margery had to wait for over three months for a suitable ship to Palestine, and during this time she made herself unpopular by breaking the

promise to her fellow passengers not to tell religious stories during meals. Her companions preferred a more normal 'merrymaking' at lunch and supper, and so they forced her to eat her meals alone in her room. We know for sure that her confessor told her that she should eat meat, but Margery refused. She appears to have stuck to her vegetarian diet (at a time when such a regime was virtually unknown and frowned upon by medical authorities) and may have sampled artichokes, which are frequently mentioned by travellers as an appealing starter. The word is among the earliest of Italian origin to be listed in the *Oxford English Dictionary*, cited from around 1531.[5]

If Venice, Bologna, Florence and Rome were natural destinations for pilgrims from northern Europe, England was a very unusual destination for an Italian humanist in the early part of the fifteenth century. But when Henry Beaufort, Bishop of Winchester and uncle of the young Henry V, asked the learned classical scholar Poggio Bracciolini – the discoverer of many works of classical antiquity – to follow him to London as his Latin secretary, Poggio accepted. But the youthful Poggio soon found himself isolated, with little money, and rather grumpy. He felt that in England he had ended up 'toiling and shivering'; the libraries were not to his liking, full of medieval books by English theologians, rather than exciting classical tomes. He was keen to visit Oxford, but never managed to do it for lack of funds. However, he told his friend Niccolò Niccoli that 'if Britain was devoid of classical treasures, it was replete with cookbooks, whose authors were "very learned".' Because of this he was becoming something of a glutton, and had a paunch to show for it. In a letter of 21 February 1421 he wrote that if one were interested in 'how many courses to prepare for a banquet or the art of making sauces, you could perhaps find some pretty good authors here, well trained for that kind of game.' However, after returning to Rome he wrote disparagingly about people who devoted their time to 'food and cookshops, or who practise cookery, neglecting all other occupations'.[6]

Who were these early gastronomes? Is it possible that Poggio actually saw manuscript cookbooks that have since been lost? Or is it all a kind of learned joke? Was he simply referring to the catalogue of 'least proper' occupations provided by Cicero in his work *De officiis* ('On duties', I.150) in which the

Roman author lists 'fishmongers, butchers, cooks, poultry vendors'? What was he getting at? Bracciolini was well known for his irony, and perhaps he felt, like other humanists, that Rome was full of foreigners attracted by the easy money one could make carrying out 'base occupations', and '*in primis* cooking'. Or maybe he was worried that the 'new learning' was going to affect even new concepts, which were found in a lighter, innovative type of cookery, later expressed in Platina's treatise, the *De honesta voluptate et valetudine* ('Of virtuous pleasure and good health'). [7]

There were later pilgrims who took greater delight in sampling foreign food than the vegetarian Margery Kempe. Sir Richard Guylford, heading for the Holy Land in 1506, went through the Alps and stopped at Alessandria in Piedmont where he was entertained by members of a prominent local family, the Pallavicinis. They showed him and his wife 'great honour' by preparing a feast during which they 'stuffed [them] with victuals, bread and wine'.[8] A decade later Sir Richard Torkington, a parson of Mulberton in Norfolk, started on his pilgrimage to the Continent, sailing from Rye in 1517 and landing in northern France.[9] He dismissed Paris rapidly, crossed the Alps and when he finally reached Pavia, he sold his horse, his saddle and his bridle. His intention was to carry on by boat. Sailing down the river Po (which he unfortunately called the 'Poo'), he finally docked at Piacenza, which happens to be my own home town.

Once there, he makes no mention in his diary of monuments, churches or relics, but instead records that 'in Placentia or Pleasance I stuffed myself with wine, bread, and other [provisions]'.[10] What could these be? The food available at that time of the year was listed in broad sheets hanging in public places, and eggs, chicken and pork were among the delicacies on offer.

Sir Richard arrived in Piacenza on 21 April, when lots of fresh vegetables, such as lettuce, carrots, celery and artichokes, would have been in season, but, unlike Margery, he was probably not interested, since he doesn't mention them at all: what featured on his plate and in his memory were the region's sausages and salamis. They would have been made by specialist butchers a few months before, during the dead of winter, and would certainly have contained local pork, a generous splash of red wine, a sprinkling of salt and a little garlic and spices, including cinnamon, cloves and mace. Then they would be left hanging in a dark cellar until they reached maturity, and were just perfect for consumption.

The area around Piacenza is still famous for its salami and other types of pork produce. The *coppa* of Piacenza, a mixture of pork loin and spices similar to what is called *capocollo* in other regions, is particularly renowned, as are the large, heavy *pancettas* of cured belly of pork. Salami made with red wine and a hint of garlic are also well known. Celtic tribes, who inhabited this part of Italy before the Etruscans and the Romans, were apparently very fond of this produce, and Italians have never lost their taste for sausages from Piacenza. In the eighteenth century the Piacentine Cardinal Giulio Alberoni wrote from Spain, where he was Prime Minister, to one of his best friends asking for a case of the local, plump salami to be shipped to Madrid, because King Philip V's consort, Queen Elisabetta (a fellow Italian who came from nearby Parma), was particularly keen on them. It was rumoured that Her Majesty could eat a whole salami in just one day![11]

When Sir Richard arrived in Venice he was invited to visit a ship that would take pilgrims to the Holy Land, and the patron provided him and his fellow travellers with 'a marvellous good dinner, where we had all manner of victuals and wines'.[12] He also went, again with a group of pilgrims, to witness a banquet held by Doge Leonardo Loredan in honour of the Marquis of Mantua. He tells us that 'there was [*sic*] eight courses of sundry meats, and at every course the trumpets and the minstrels came in before them'. Sir Richard was suitably impressed by what followed: 'and when the dinner was done, the Duke sent to the pilgrims great basins full of marchpanes and also comfits and malmsey, and other sweet wines, as much as any man would eat and drink'.[13] One of the sweet wines may have been a local *vin santo*, literally 'holy wine', used during the celebration of the Catholic mass, or an early example of the best dessert wine from the Veneto region, such as Torcolato.

Marchpane, or marzipan, would certainly have been a novelty. It derives from Arabic, and originally referred to a ceramic box in which sweet confections made of almond paste and sugar were kept. The origin of this food speciality was the city of Martaban (now Mottama) in South Burma/Myanmar, and like many oriental spices and sweetmeats probably spread through the West via Venice; some wrappings of marzipan carried the stamp of St Mark's lion, the symbol of Venice (occasioning one theory, but not one to which I subscribe, that the name evolved from a Latin phrase, *Marci pane*, 'the bread of St Mark'). Marzipan is mentioned in an Italian document of 1337, and *marchpane* is first recorded in English just one year before Sir

Richard Torkington began his travels. The *Oxford English Dictionary* provides the following definition: 'originally: a flat disc of marzipan mounted on wafers and usually decorated with motifs made from similar paste or other materials'. The second occurrence noted by the *OED* and dated 1517, comes from Torkington's own diary. By the end of the century it was sufficiently well known for Shakespeare to have a Capulet servant asking to be saved 'a piece of marchpane' just moments before Romeo sets eyes on Juliet.

The diary of Sir Richard was printed as late as 1883, but we do know of at least two handwritten copies made in the sixteenth and seventeenth centuries, which indicates that stories based on foreign travels were gaining slightly more attention in England.

SPILLING THE BEANS

Obtaining information about Italian food before visiting the country was not easy for English travellers, although treatises in English concerning dietary prescriptions largely derived from classical authors or from ancient Arab writers were available. One such dietary was penned by a physician and a former Carthusian monk, Andrew Borde (or Boorde, *c.*1490–1549), who was rumoured to be 'uncomfortable with the abstemious, vegetarian lifestyle of the cloistered Carthusians' and hence asked to be released of his vows.[14]

Borde was familiar with continental Europe, having lived and studied in Montpellier. In his writings, he summarily describes Venice, Lombardy, Florence, Genoa, Rome and Sicily. His vision of Italy is that of a wealthy country, with fertile ground and plenty of oil, wine, bread, corn and fruit. Borde also remarks on the inhabitants of the various regions. His comments perhaps were aimed at helping merchants intending to go to Italy on business. The locals are at times described as 'subtle and crafty' and the Lombards strike him as having some unusual eating habits. He claims that people there will eat frogs, guts and all, and he adds that snakes, snails and mushrooms were considered delicious.[15]

(above) Quinces
(previous) Vincenzo Campi, *Fruit Seller*, oil on canvas, 1578–81

of a very high colour, Vernaccia, a strong heady wine, Romanesco, which is drunk for a delicate wine in winter, Latino, which is a delicate small wine for summer', and diverse others.[24] Incidentally, Dante mentions Vernaccia di San Gimignano (which is still highly prized today) in connection with the gluttony of Pope Martin IV, who was rumoured to drown eels in Vernaccia before roasting and eating them.[25]

In the Kingdom of Naples, Sir Thomas found a vast choice of wheat, barley and all other grains in a very fertile country with abundant water springs. He also described a rare and precious sugary substance, produced by the crystallized sap of certain species of ash trees.[26] It had substantial commercial value and was used in medicine and confectionery, and was referred to as *manna*, after the life-giving substance that, according to the Bible, fed the Israelites in the wilderness.

It is fascinating to see how the image of Italy changes in the middle of the sixteenth century, when English gentlemen back from their travels start to spread information about life in various parts of the peninsula. At this time a few Italians also reached London in flight from the Inquisition. Some would become teachers of Italian, and others preachers; the sceptical Roger Ascham was among those who suspected that Londoners did not flock to hear their sermons as such but just to listen to the 'musical language'.[27] Italy was becoming fashionable but the English were not quite ready to adopt authentic Italian cuisine; they were more partial to an *interpretation* of Italian cooking. An English gentleman, Sir Hugh Plat (1552–1608) did advocate the use of pasta as a naval victual, eminently suitable for long voyages,[28] but with the exception of the *Epulario, or the Italian Banquet*,[29] very few Italian cookery books were known at this time.

The *Epulario*, published in London in 1598, was the translation, and most likely the only one of its kind, of a work by Giovanni Rosselli, who in the Italian original oddly declares himself to be French! After a basic discussion of what kinds of meat are more suitable for roasting or boiling, there follows a collection of recipes. Many dishes came from manuscripts dating back more than a century earlier, by the great cook Maestro Martino de' Rossi, whom we have already met in the previous chapter. The text is fairly accurate, although at times the translator seems to have difficulty with names of Italian recipes, and decides not to mention 'macaroni' or 'vermicelli' but talks of 'flour meals' instead. Many dishes listed in the Italian original are accompanied by strong sauces and much garlic, but the translator cannot bring himself to mention the 'g' word and a chicken which is supposed to be stuffed with the bulbous plant goes without!

A few years later, Sir Thomas Palmer wrote about the advantages of travelling abroad in acquiring knowledge of the laws and customs of foreign countries, as well as of their diet, specifying five reasons – including climate, education and 'variable manners and inclinations of the people, to civility and humanity' – why it was worth visiting Italy.[30] But even people who did not travel abroad were ordering food items from Italy if they were wealthy enough to do so: Sir Arthur Throckmorton is recorded as having bought 2lb of capers, a gallon of Genoa olives, a gallon of great olives and 3lb of anchovies, while similar provisions, including 6lb of capers and 'one pound case of nutmegs', were sent for by Lord Howard of Naworth in Cumberland.[31]

In the early seventeenth century the polymath Gervase Markham published *The English Hus-wife*, a manual addressed to women and including a number of recipes, some of which were inspired by Italy, even if he warned about the danger of the 'ideal housewife' being influenced by fashions from 'other countries'. Some recipes come straight from the medieval tradition, such as the sweet almond and cinnamon concoction *leche lumbard*, while *paste of Genoa* was probably a Renaissance invention, usually made with baked quinces, well pounded in a mortar with sugar, cinnamon, ginger and some Damask rosewater 'till it come to a stiff paste'.[32] Otherwise, recipes inspired by Italy were generally still sparse before the middle of the seventeenth century.

SHOPPING AND DINING OUT IN ITALY

A special mention should go to Fynes Morison or Moryson (1565/6–1630), the son of a gentleman from Lincolnshire and a seasoned traveller. He studied at Peterhouse, Cambridge, and won a fellowship there before devoting ten years of his life to visiting various European countries. On his return to England in 1601, he prepared an impressive, multi-volume diary recounting his long journey through Europe. However, only a limited number of volumes were published, in 1617.[33]

Moryson has plenty to offer us, and he is obviously keen to provide useful information to fellow travellers. He comments on the eating habits of various Italian cities. For example, 'the Florentines are of spare diet, but wonderful cleanliness. Those of Lucca keep golden mediocrity in all things'; 'those of Genoa are of most spare diet and no cleanliness. The Mantuans feed on base beans'[34] while 'the Milanese live plentifully, and provoke appetite with sharp sauces'.[35] No doubt, once again, with lots of garlic.[36] According to him, Italians did not eat as much meat as the people of northern Europe and they were happy with a piece of bread and a basket full of salad vegetables dressed with a little olive oil. He praised the excellent white bread and the fact that it was frequently eaten with 'roots', by which I suspect he meant leeks and onions as well as turnips, white carrots and radishes.[37]

Moryson is the first traveller to reveal what Italians ate for breakfast: a slice of cake or sweet bread (called *pasta reale*, *ciambolini* or more generally *gentilezze*) and a cup of sweet wine.[38] According to him this was a way of avoiding lunch. Maybe what he calls a 'spare diet' was more common than we think. However, like many other travellers he describes how plentiful food was in the markets of Venice. There one could find 'mutton, veal, sold in little portions and by weight' – he notes that spits are not used to roast meat, since the Italians prefer stews in earthen pots. He also remarks on plenty of fish, hens, eggs, Turkey hens, pickled herrings, caviar and 'botargo' (*bottarga*, mullet or tuna roe); hard cheese, mushrooms, snails and frogs' legs, were all considered real treats and could be found in abundance because 'the common sort eat little or no flesh, or fish, or birds, but only herbs, pulses, snails, roots and white bread'.[39] At this time there was a theory, known as 'the great chain of being', which provided a hierarchical structure of what each social class should eat, according to their station. Therefore people who ploughed the soil

Luis Melendez, *The Afternoon Meal (La Merienda)*, oil on canvas, c.1772
(overleaf) Giovanna Garzoni, *Still Life with Bowl of Citrons*, tempera on vellum, late 1640s

[they] had paid seven bolinei, a pound of figs at the same price, and a pound of almonds at the same price, bought at Ferrara for this purpose'.[44] They consumed the same ingredients when they had to ride for most of the day, with the addition of a flask of wine.

Apropos of wine, one of the most celebrated travellers of the time, Thomas Coryat (c.1577–1617), a character well known at court as a jester and a wit, and much appreciated by young Henry, Prince of Wales, learnt the hard way about drinking Italian wine. He suffered a terrible tummy upset after crossing the Alps from France, when he had enjoyed drinking, probably in large quantities, 'the sweet wines' of Piedmont. He therefore recommended that anybody arriving in Italy should mix their wine with water, as the Italians did. This practice is quite familiar to me too. Both my grandfather and my father drank almost exclusively wine at meal times, but they always diluted it. The everyday wine they consumed at home was usually bought direct from the vineyard owners, who were family acquaintances. Most of the time the grapes were pressed 'manually', that is to say by foot. Jumping up and down in a large wooden tub, and seeing the red must pouring out into buckets, was a kind of joyous ritual in the autumn, and one I was allowed to take part in once I was eight or nine. I did so with great enthusiasm and I still remember the beautiful ruby colour of my legs afterwards. I later had a generous taste of the fermented juice, but that is a different story.

Treading the grapes was a time-honoured but crude method of making wine, and in his *Crudities, Hastily Gobbled in Five Months' Travels* (1611), Thomas Coryat paid attention to both food and drink.[45] He was one of the first to complain about the use of grated cheese over most of the Italian dishes he was served, a practice he did not like (although Sir Philip Skippon, who also remarked upon it some fifty years later, was not averse). However, he enjoyed a dish of fried frogs, which he knew were used in various parts of Italy. He added that they were 'curiously dressed' but they delighted his palate.

Many early travellers seemed obsessed with the novelty of frogs, which in Italy were enjoyed by most people, from peasants to popes. A book of bilingual dialogues – Italian and English – for travelling contemporaries of Coryat features a fictitious conversation (aiming to distinguish good food from bad) in which a question about eating snails and frogs is posed. The convoluted answer points out that snails were excellent for sufferers of consumption and frogs 'a panacea against the poison of all serpents'.[46] In about a hundred pages of dialogues, the book covers all manner of food, from salads to meat and game, cheese and cardoons, throwing light on which foods were popular.

When Coryat reached the north-east of Italy, near Lake Garda, he noted a great quantity of oranges, lemons, citrus and apricots, and he was especially struck by the variety of melons: musk melons (Cantaloupe), *anguriae* (watermelons) and others with different colours, especially yellow and green. In Venice he noticed that the melons were brought to the market morning and evening, and although he found them all quite delicious and refreshing, he warned about the danger of eating too much of a good thing. Melons were, according to him, 'sweet to the palate but sour for the stomach', and potentially dangerous. Pope Paul II apparently died from severe indigestion in 1471, after eating too much melon, and Coryat himself claims that the Emperor Frederick III passed away in a similar fashion.[47]

As he moved away from Venice, Coryat remarked on the fertile land with good meadows and pastures between Vicenza and Verona, but also a scarcity of sheep, which, in his view, were necessary for the 'sustentation of man's life'.

PIZZA AND PASTA BUT NOT QUITE AS WE KNOW THEM...

Unlike later travellers and scholars, Thomas Coryat, although fascinated by the abundance of fruit, was not much interested in vegetables, and, like many others, he does not mention what is considered a modern staple of Italian cooking: pasta.[48] It is hard to believe now but this was not a common dish at inns and probably not in private houses either. Even Richard Lassels, who recorded eating habits and quirks in great detail in his *The Voyage of*

Juan Sanchez Cotan, *Still Life with a Cardoon and Francolin*, oil on canvas, 1628

56

Italy (1670), doesn't mention pasta.[49] Many pasta dishes would become significantly popular only in the nineteenth century.

The fact that we find numerous recipes for pasta dishes in Italian fifteenth- and sixteenth-century books does not mean that they were widely available. Such preparations invariably involved a certain amount of time and expertise, and recipe collections are generally representative of cooking for the higher and wealthier echelons of society. Although some of our travellers, such as Sir Thomas Hoby, mingled with aristocrats, others, including Moryson, moved in much humbler circles.

Yet some pasta dishes, or at least the names for them, had reached England, and we find them in the first ever Italian–English dictionary, entitled *A World of Words* (1598). Its author, John Florio, was the son of a Tuscan pastor who had fled to London in 1550 because of his Protestant faith.[50] Numerous Italian literary works provided Florio with vocabulary for foods and cookery terms, but the works of a literary acquaintance of his, William Shakespeare, proved no use for English equivalents, as so few were mentioned!

Among the Italian foods Florio mentions, we find entries for *crostata*, *gnocchi*, *lasagne*, *maccaroni*, *pappardelle*, *rafiuoli*, *tagliarelli* and *vermicelli*.[51] The explanation he provides for *pizza* is somewhat unexpected: after defining it as 'any kind of itch, scurf, … tetter, or ring-worm', Florio adds 'also a kind of rugged cake or simnel-bread or wafer. Also a kind of sugar tart'.[52] It is true that in an earlier recipe book, pizza is essentially a tart made with layers of pasta and melted butter, sugar and fresh or dried elderflowers, baked in the oven, and served with extra sugar and rosewater on top.[53] For the pizza we know and love today, we have to wait a little longer.

Thanks to Florio, some members of the upper classes became true Italophiles. From being 'great lovers of themselves [who] think that there are no other men than themselves, and no other world but England',[54] they followed in Elizabeth I's footsteps and learnt Italian as well as Latin, and believed that mastering those languages was the key to fully understanding and appreciating Classical civilization.

The *World of Words* lists numerous vegetables and herbs from artichokes, chicory and the cure-all herb 'panacea',[55] to parsnip and *zucca* (translated as

Main kitchen, from Bartolomeo Scappi, *Opera*, Venice: Michele Tramezzino, 1570

CARDOONS WITH PARMESAN CHEESE

Serves 6
3kg (6lb) cardoons
400g (14oz) freshly grated Parmesan
5–6 tbsp extra virgin olive oil
1 tbsp fine breadcrumbs
lemon juice

Clean the stems to remove all the leaves and the toughest fibres. Cut them into pieces about 2–3cm (1in) long, put them in some water, add some lemon juice to avoid them getting black, and boil them in salted water for about 50 minutes or an hour. Drain and leave to cool.

Butter an ovenproof dish and cover the bottom with some of the cardoon stems in a single, close-fitting layer. Cover with a generous quantity of the Parmesan and a sprinkling of olive oil. Continue to build more layers – you should get a minimum of three, possibly four, layers – to make a kind of cardoon lasagne. Over the final layer, sprinkle more Parmesan and the breadcrumbs, as well as a couple of spoons of oil, with a little salt and pepper if necessary. Bake it at 180°C (350°F, gas mark 4) for at least 45 minutes, until a delicious crust has formed on top. The dish is better eaten warm, not hot, and can be used as a starter, as an accompaniment, or indeed as a main vegetarian course. It is excellent reheated the day after, or even after two days.

I cannot imagine Castelvetro's food choices to have been an instant hit among children, not then, not now. But he did mention a sweet treat that might appeal to kids. Well, just. We are not talking triple chocolate brownies but a kind of sweet, wobbly pudding made with fresh grape must boiled with flour and sugar. Actually, *súgoli*, as he calls them, were something I used to eat myself when I was small.[61] I have recently come across them in Italian supermarkets but, alas, the mass-produced flavour is a far cry from my childhood's memory. The version opposite is based on my mother's recipe.

Castelvetro's work was preserved in at least four manuscript copies either written by him or under his supervision, but it is likely that his eccentric views enjoyed only limited circulation in England. A vegetarian diet was still considered unfit for a posh table in Britain, and certainly not top of a list of dietary ingredients. But things were about to change. At least, a little.

SÚGOLI

Serves 6
1kg (2lb) sweet black grapes
120ml (4fl oz) water
100g (4oz) caster sugar
70g (3oz) wheat flour
vanilla pod or a few drops of vanilla extract

Remove the grapes from the stems, and wash them thoroughly. Put the grapes in a pan, cover and heat through gently for 3–4 minutes. Add water and stir. Cover the pan and continue simmering, stirring from time to time, for about 15 minutes.

Remove the mushy grapes and pass them through a mouli sieve, to remove the skins. Reserve the juice.

Mix the sugar and flour well in a bowl, add the seeds of vanilla or the vanilla extract. Then add the grape juice little by little to the sugar and flour mixture, using a whisk to obtain a smooth, thick purée.

Pour the purée into a pan and bring slowly to the boil.

When the grape juice has reached the consistency of a thick jelly, with a distinctive purple colour, remove the pan from the heat. Leave to cool slightly.

Divide the mixture equally into six ramekins. Cover them and chill in the fridge for at least one hour.

3. ADVENTURES IN THE SEVENTEENTH CENTURY AND BEYOND

WHEN I WAS AT PRIMARY SCHOOL I would often spend lazy summer afternoons on a remote farm, perched in my favourite mulberry tree, sometimes exploring the surrounding countryside through binoculars. When I had had enough, I would climb down, drink a couple of glasses of beautifully cool spring water, and go into the vegetable patch to relish the fragrant sweetness of small freshly picked peas; my *nonna*, who spent many hours working there, would teach me about wild plants, as well as the ones she cultivated, such as green, red and yellow peppers, aubergines, broad beans, chickpeas and fennel.

With the exception of peppers, all the others were cherished by one of my favourite seventeenth-century British writers and travellers: John Evelyn (1620–1706). He would have wholeheartedly approved of my lifestyle, my passion for vegetables, and my childhood earthly paradise where lunch always started with a delicious minestrone soup made with fresh borlotti beans, or some spaghetti with roughly chopped tomatoes whose sweetness coated my lips.

To this day Evelyn remains an extraordinary character. He came from a family who had made a fortune from gunpowder, though he himself never hurt a fly, a man with enlightened views on the natural world and a passionate pioneer of one of the first green movements. He was a keen gardener and an advocate of landscape gardening, and what we would label today an environmentalist.[1] He went on to become one of the founding members of the Royal Society. Evelyn is best known for his monumental *Diary*, although he wrote a large number of important scientific books as well.[2]

Evelyn lived through the English Civil War and the Restoration, but always managed to pursue peaceful activities and was deeply committed to the condemnation of animal cruelty.[3] He travelled extensively, and spent a few years in Italy, where he developed his ideas concerning a vegetarian diet.[4]

Even in his student days at Balliol College, Oxford, Evelyn had an interest in what nowadays we would call international cuisine. One day in 1637, a Greek undergraduate by the name of Nathaniel Conopios started brewing something that Evelyn had never smelt before: '[he] was the first that I ever saw drink *Caffè*, not heard of then in England'.[5] The aroma of this new brew had reached the student lodgings at Balliol about two decades before the first coffee houses opened in the town.

After his travels in Italy Evelyn wrote a book wholly devoted to salad vegetables called *Acetaria. A Discourse of Sallets* [salads].[6] It was published in 1699 and originally envisaged as part of an ambitious encyclopaedia on plants and the use of vegetables. Evelyn states that 'the more frugal Italians and French, to this day, accept and gather *ogni verdura*, any thing almost that's green and tender, to the very top of nettles'.[7] In spring I too often go foraging for nettles to turn them into a delicious bright green soup, excellent for detoxing.

NETTLE SOUP

Serves 2

1 onion, chopped

1 clove garlic, roughly chopped

400g (1lb) washed nettle tops (NB wear rubber gloves
when handling the nettles)

1 medium potato, peeled and chopped into small chunks

1.5 litres (2½pt) vegetable or chicken stock (or water)

olive oil

salt and pepper

100ml (4 fl oz) single cream (optional)

a little yoghurt and handful of croutons, to serve

In a large pan, sweat the onion in the oil, then add the garlic and, after a
minute or so, the nettle tops, potato and stock or water. Season. Simmer for
about 30 minutes. Whizz the soup in a blender, check the seasoning and serve
it with a drizzle or dollop of yoghurt and some croutons. If you want a richer
soup, just add some single cream before taking the pan off the stove.

Evelyn's own mantra was that 'every hedge affords a sallet'.[8] He advised seasoning the salad leaves with just the right amount of vinegar, salt and olive oil – even better, he said, if the oil came from the Tuscan countryside around Lucca.[9] He considered raw dandelions 'very wholesome' dressed with oil and vinegar, to which, personally I would add a hint of raw garlic, an ingredient that was forbidden in Evelyn's salads 'by reason of its intolerable rankness';[10] however, a 'light touch on the dish, with a clove [of garlic]' was at times acceptable, even desirable to add a hidden depth.[11]

In *Acetaria*, Evelyn provides a detailed table for the composition of salads, suggesting the quantity of each ingredient, depending on the season. In dealing with the main vegetables, listed alphabetically, he frequently refers to the practice of Italian cooks.[12] Artichokes, for instance, when young and tender can be cut in quarters and eaten raw, and dressed with oil, a little vinegar, salt and pepper, but they can also be fried in butter with a sprinkling of parsley. Or, if the leaves are tough, they can be boiled, and their hearts can be 'baked in pies, with marrow, dates and other rich ingredients'. He adds that in Italy they sometimes 'broil' them, that is they expose them to the fierce heat of red-hot embers. When the scaly leaves open, they are basted 'with fresh and sweet oil' and eaten with orange juice and sugar.[13] According to Evelyn the cultivation of this 'noble thistle' in Italy had improved its size and quality, and he laments the fact that they are 'so rare in England, that they were commonly sold for crowns a piece'.[14] Indeed, they can be difficult to find in some parts of Britain even today, and some professionals may not be familiar with them. I remember an acquaintance who, when asked to prepare a private dinner only a few years ago, had to send for help because he had never dealt with a globe artichoke before.[15]

The Jerusalem artichoke (*Helianthus tuberosus*) is also mentioned by Evelyn as 'a new discovery' and was slightly more commonly found. It is said to derive its name from *girasole*, the Italian for 'sunflower', and arrived in England in 1613 from North America via the Dutch port of Terneuzen. Evelyn records that he once made 'macaroons with the ripe blanched seeds [tubers], but the turpentine did so domineer over all, that it did not answer expectation'.[16]

The vegetable that probably had the greatest success in the long run in England was '*broccoli* from Naples … agreeable to most palates' according to Evelyn, and also recommended by the Reverend John Swinton on a visit to Genoa in 1731: 'so tender and fine-tasting that no greens in England or elsewhere can come up to it'.[17] Evelyn was also keen on fennel, known as Florence fennel, although for him the best came from Bologna. Its virtues, he wrote, were to sharpen the sight and 'recreate the brain'.[18] In a mid eighteenth-century manuscript I came across 'white Endive or white fennell', followed by a recipe for a fennel salad in which the core of a fennel is boiled until tender then served 'with a few currents, & a little sliced ginger and oyle & vinegar or butter. You may pickle them up in winter to be a sallet.'[19]

Although Evelyn lists over seventy herbs, vegetables and edible flowers, there is no mention of an exotic plant that had been discovered in South

America in the mid sixteenth century, imported to Spain, and which arrived at the court of the Duke of Tuscany in Pisa in 1548: the tomato.[20] This fleshy fruit remained a botanical rarity, suspected of being poisonous, and reached aristocratic Italian tables only in the 1690s. In England it was mentioned by Philip Miller, gardener to London's eighteenth-century apothecaries, who described in his *Gardeners Dictionary* certain varieties of tomatoes used in Spain, Italy and Portugal for the production of soups, sauces and salads.[21]

In the seventeenth century and later, the debate about human diet was frequently mixed with theological arguments and with scientific, or pseudo-scientific, views, and many maintained that it was actually necessary to eat animal flesh for survival. Evelyn never declared himself a vegetarian, or a follower of the 'hortulan diet' as he called it (relating to the kitchen garden, from the Latin *hortus*); he simply preferred vegetables, and advocated them

Cheese is not mentioned specifically in customs registers, but it is likely that Parmesan travelled south by road from Lodi, Piacenza or Parma to the nearest port (probably Genoa) and then on to an Italian or English ship heading for Dover or London. The journey took approximately a month but Parmesan cheese travels quite well, and can mature for long periods of time, two years and even longer. Richard Lassels, an earlier traveller, wrote that some cheeses from Lombardy were exceedingly large, and near Lodi he had seen 'cheeses as big as millstones', and heard that some of them could weigh up to 500lb![27]

The fame of Lodi and Parmesan cheese is celebrated, as an excellent substitute for desserts, in a poem of the era attributed to Dr Walter Pope:

In lieu of des[s]erts, unwholesome and dear,
Let Lodi or Parmesan bring up the rear.[28]

This was repeated by Mrs Hester Lynch Piozzi, a traveller of whom we shall hear more later, when she reached Lodi from Milan, 'a place renowned through all Europe for its excellent cheese, as our well-known ballad bears testimony: "Let Lodi or Parmesan bring up the rear."'[29]

Just like his Parmesan, Pepys and his friends luckily managed to avoid the worst of the fire and decided to sup on 'a shoulder of mutton' albeit 'without any napkin or any thing, in a sad manner' but still in good spirits.[30] We do not know if the Parmesan was dug up again after the Great Fire of London, but I am pretty sure that both wine and cheese ended up on someone's table.

When Robert May compiled his *The Accomplisht Cook*, first published in 1660, he included a substantial number of Italian recipes – May had spent a long time in France and knew Spanish and Italian, and his work was certainly influential.[31] A few recipes he had collected include the use of Parmesan, such as the one for 'Capitolado' in which some minced veal is mixed with two pounds of grated Parmesan, and ten cloves of garlic.[32] May's book also included a detailed description of 'Bolonia sausages' which, he instructed, should preferably be prepared in September. Then there were recipes for 'land fowls or birds', such as a pigeon 'in the Italian fashion, in a broth called Brodo Lardiero' (a broth popular at the time, which would typically have been made with venison poached in wine).[33] There are pottages and other dishes 'in the Italian fashion' as well as 'little pasties, called in Italian *Tortelleti*'.

Numerous recipes, including 'Italian minced pies in the Italian fashion',[34] are indebted to Bartolomeo Scappi's great sixteenth-century book of recipes, but the source of a recipe for a spice mixture 'called *Tamara* in Italian' seems to be unknown. Támara is recorded with the meaning of 'dried date' in Italian, probably from Portuguese and ultimately from an Arab term. The recipe May supplies could be defined as a condiment of 'warm' mixed spices:

> To make this *Tamara*, take two ounces of coriander seed, an ounce of aniseed, an ounce of fennel-seed, two ounces of cloves, and an ounce of cinnamon, beat them into a gross powder with a little powder of winter savory and put them in a viol glass to keep.[35]

ITALIAN WAREHOUSES

Pepys's Parmesan gives us a clue that specialized grocers already existed in the late seventeenth century in the British capital, and by around 1720 we find shops in central London known as 'Italian warehouses'.[36] They were mostly concentrated in the Strand, just west of Fleet Street and the City, and remained so into the nineteenth century. At the beginning of his poem *Beppo: A Venetian Story* (1817), Byron recommends a 'walk or ride to the Strand' to procure 'ketchup, soy, chili-vinegar, and Harvey', and his readers would have most certainly understood which shops he meant.

Some of these emporia derived from the so-called 'oilmen shops' which sold spermaceti oil for lamps, wax and tallow candles, as well as olive oil, pickles and exotic sauces. Burgess's at 107 Strand was one such, claiming descent from the oilman's shop set up by John Burgess around 1760. Surviving early advertisements and trade cards give an idea of what the Italian warehouses stocked; the following came framed in an elegant engraving inspired by Italian Classical motifs (see illustration, page 89):

At Mrs Holts, Italian Ware House at ye two Olive Posts in ye Broad part
of the Strand almost opposite to Exeter Change are sold all sorts of Italian
Silks, ... Fans, Leghorn Hats ... And in a Back Ware house all Sorts of Italian
wines, Florence Cordials, Oyl, Olives, Anchovies, Capers, Vermicelli, Bolognia
Sausidges, Parmesan Cheeses, Naple soap &c.[37]

Mrs Holt offered vermicelli but pasta was still not a major feature of Italian
cuisine in Britain. William Verrall, the author of *A Complete System of Cookery*
(1759), often mentions vermicelli, but macaroni, which he describes as 'a
foreign paste, the same as vermicelli, but made very large', was still considered
a novelty. He provides two recipes, one with cream and one with Parmesan
cheese.[38] Vermicelli continued to be the most recognizable name for pasta into
the nineteenth century.

By the mid eighteenth century, 'Italian' had clearly become a synonym for exotic and intriguing produce, with an increasing interest in Italian food among the affluent classes.[39] The flourishing trade between Italian ports and London, Southampton, Dover or Bristol, combined with well-established Italian warehouses, proves that foreign delicatessens were in demand. A certain Isabella Pease, in a manuscript dated May 1759, provides an intriguing recipe for an 'Italian cheese', most probably a type of sour cream.

ITALIAN CHEESE

[Take] a pint of thick cream the rind of a lemon [g]rated and the juice, mix all well together, [sw]eeten it to your taste, whisk it half an [ho]ur, then have ready a tin to put it in, [w]ith a piece of ga[u]ze over it, put it by [spo]onfuls off the top and let it stand all [nig]ht.[40]

The designation 'oil and Italian warehouse' was still common in London in the early decades of the nineteenth century. By this time some were decidedly upmarket, such as Mackay & Co. of Piccadilly, who during the Regency period described themselves as 'Oilmen, Purveyors of Truffles &c, to H.M. and H.R.H. the Prince of Wales' and in the 1830s, under the label of Sherborn & Sams, Mackay & Co., as 'Oilmen to His Majesty, Importers of Italian & other Foreign Goods'.[41] One of the best known competitors to these shops was Fortnum & Mason of Piccadilly, which started trading in 1707, and is still very much in business today.

Occasionally 'Indian and Italian warehouse' would appear, especially after the return of British officers from the colonies, and an establishment near Leicester Square kept by 'Signor Pagliano' was recommended in 1815 as 'a reasonable house for getting a good dinner, either in the French, English or Italian style'.[42]

By the 1820s, Ambrose Peck's Italian warehouse, at 175 Strand, near Somerset House, was a more upmarket grocer's shop than the one run by John Peck approximately fifty years earlier. Here, wealthy customers could find 'India Soy, Espagnole Sauce, Quin Sauce, Compleat Boxes of Rich Fish Sauces, Sauce Piquant, Sauce Royal, Harvey's Sauce, Cherokee Sauce', as well as 'Walnut Ketchup, Essence [of] Anchovies, Lemon Pickle, Curry Powders, Capers, Olives, Vinegar, Salt Prunella' (the last a now obsolete chemical term referring to nitre prepared in little balls).[43] I was struck by the name of the owner, who may be connected with the most famous delicatessen in Milan: Peck, sited in the very central Via Spadari. The shop has been selling charcuterie, cheeses and all sorts of delicacies since 1883.

Italian warehouses could also be found outside the capital, in Bristol, Cardiff, Edinburgh, Glasgow, Pool, Totnes, and in other towns. In Oxford there was one shop in the Cornmarket, selling oranges and lemons, Sheard's Italian Warehouse in the High Street, selling oil and vinegar (bought in from Domenico Piccirillo's specialist Italian firm in Soho), and later on came the most renowned of them all, Frank Cooper, well known for the marmalade produced by his wife Sarah, and which remained in existence until 1919.[44]

CASANOVA AND HIS SEARCH FOR A SPOONFUL OF 'MINESTRA'

One could enjoy 'delicious meals' in eighteenth-century London, even if restaurants had not been invented,[45] and one to say so is Giacomo Casanova.[46]

The great adventurer and traveller spent nearly a year in London, where he arrived in June 1763, and his first impressions of the island called 'Angleterre' was that everything that was eaten there tasted differently from what he was used to.[47]

He rented a house in Pall Mall, in the middle of town, together with the services of an English chef, who cooked him excellent roast beef, as well as French dishes.[48] Casanova claimed that the English were mutton-eaters,[49] not interested in bread nor a little soup at the start of a meal because it was considered too expensive, since nobody, allegedly, would eat the beef used to make the broth – even though he, Casanova, found English salt beef excellent.[50] But Casanova could not do without his *minestra* (soup) and since this was not provided in the local taverns, he preferred to eat at home. The same went for drinking: he found English beer far too bitter, but luckily 'natural' excellent French wines, though expensive, were available from good wine merchants.[51]

And despite the cost, when he gave a party for twelve people in his apartments, he and his guests drank their way through forty bottles of wine![52]

When Casanova ordered a snack at the theatre for some friends, a few green oysters were quickly provided. However, having realized that his companions were actually hungry, he immediately ordered everything the place had to offer, including a young hare, which, according to him, was only available in London at the tables of very wealthy people.[53] The meal went on for one and a half hours, and the waiter served plenty of champagne, liqueurs, rare little birds such as larks and figpeckers,[54] truffles and sweetmeats. Casanova, who was used to treating money with a certain nonchalance, was nevertheless taken aback when the waiter ('le *Weter*'), showing him the menu prices, said that he had to pay ten guineas. That would be over £600 in today's money.

ENGLISHWOMEN ABROAD

Despite there having been more male than female British travellers, the contribution of women to writing about Italian food should not be underestimated. It was in fact accounts from women travellers that formed the basis of Murrays and Baedeckers, the most famous commercial guides to mainland Europe. *Letters from Italy*, for example, by the traveller and writer Mariana Starke (1761/2–1838), not only enjoyed a second edition but was also translated into German.[55]

Many aristocratic women spent long periods of time in Italy, and kept diaries or correspondence which were later published in England, and sometimes in America too, where they were met with considerable success. Food and drink were and still are considered aesthetically inferior subjects to, say, paintings and sculptures, but they 'ingeniously manag[ed] the incipient intensity of aesthetic pleasure by merging this pleasure with innocent gastronomic gratification'.[56]

(facing) Maria Margaretha van Os, *Still Life with Lemon and Cut Glass*, oil on panel, 1823–6
(previous) Annibale Carracci, *The Butcher's Shop*, oil on canvas, c.1580

Henrietta Louisa Fermor, Countess of Pomfret, stayed in Italy between 1738 and 1741, and during that time corresponded extensively with her friend Frances, Countess of Hertford. Apart from writing about art and some juicy gossip, the letters contain plenty of remarks about inns and food. Henrietta Louisa told her confidante that she found dinner at Padua to her satisfaction, and that 'we found our inn airy and clean, and have dined so well that I should not be sorry to stay a day or two in it, if I had any acquaintance here.'

The countess enjoyed other good meals while travelling from Rome north towards Foligno, and in the middle of the Apennines she was greeted with a quite unexpected welcome: 'in a little house on the very highest of these eminences we ate some eggs and fish, and drank very good wine.' But, alas, in Ferrara and in Bologna things took a different turn: the inns were rather unsatisfactory, and the supper in Ferrara was not to her taste. However, moving towards Verona, the landscape and the general atmosphere improved, and Henrietta Louisa took great pleasure in admiring the river Po which reminded her 'of the Thames a little above London'. Finally, on reaching Verona, the city 'appeared more noble and beautiful that I can find words to describe. Our inn is large; and considering that we are in Italy, we have supped well'.[57]

Her critical remark did not go unnoticed by her friend. The Countess of Hertford's reply was swift and *au point*. She hoped that her letter would find Henrietta 'in some inn' waiting for her supper 'which my lord Hertford and Lord Brooke tell me seldom (through all Italy) affords any greater dainties than a *mezzo piccioni* [sic] *per testa* [half a pigeon a head] and a piece of veal'.[58] Italian food was clearly talked about among the high society in London, albeit in a slightly harsh fashion. However, it had also been remarked by other travellers that Italian pigeons were much bigger than their English counterparts. Perhaps the Countess of Hertford's comment is not so derogatory after all.

The quality and appeal of lunches and dinners varied throughout the peninsula, as the poet and salon hostess Lady Anna Miller found out for herself when she reached Viterbo on her travels in 1771. Her supper 'consisted of a soup, the chief ingredients of which were all sorts of livers and gizzards,

G.A. De Predis (attrib.), *Girl with Cherries*, oil on wood, c.1491–5

82

collected from various birds, and I believe were of as various dates, sailing after each other in a muddy pool; very unlike the lake of Bolsena; broiled pigeons with oil, and a friture of livers, etc.'[59] In all honesty who could blame her? Too many trimmings can spoil a dinner. But she might also have been writing for effect under the influence of the acerbic prose of Tobias Smollett, a rather morose traveller.[60] Her *Letters from Italy*, however, 'enjoyed some reputation', and a second edition appeared in 1777.[61] Lady Anna was at times homesick while travelling, and was only too pleased whenever she could find English food. This was gradually becoming more common in Italian cities, and she satisfied her cravings for comfort food in Florence where she found 'excellent British minced pies', while in Rome she went for something more substantial and bought 'bacon and cabbage, boiled mutton, bread-puddings'.[62]

Female travellers were by and large sent into a spin by the use of olive oil, which reminds us of the attitude expressed about a hundred years later in Mrs Beeton's *Book of Household Management*, first published in 1861: 'With us, it is principally used in mixing a salad, and when thus employed, it tends to prevent fermentation, and is an antidote against flatulency.'[63]

Melted butter was just as bad: 'many English ladies and delicate youths complain of the food, and manner of cooking it; and turn up their noses, and express their disgust at seeing pure melted butter brought to table.'[64] Garlic, as Evelyn and company had already pointed out, was singled out as a particularly objectionable ingredient in a great number of dishes. Among the most vociferous garlic haters was the Italophile poet Percy Bysshe Shelley, who was simply disgusted by Italian women who enjoyed the offensive substance with gleeful abandon.[65]

However, other English ladies were less fussy and more appreciative of hearty flavours. When Margaret, Viscountess Spencer stopped at Novara in northern Italy she had 'a true Italian breakfast consisting of the large Italian pigeons and tripe dressed with oil and Parmesan cheese, grapes, figs, and an excellent polenta which is a kind of pudding made of the flour of Indian wheat mixed with oil and cheese'.[66]

Since this is one of the earliest eighteenth-century mentions of *polenta*, I shall tell you how I make it.[67]

POLENTA

Serves 6

2 tsp salt

1.5 litre (2½pts) water

300g (11oz) pre-cooked maize flour

20g (1oz) butter

2 tbsp freshly grated Parmesan

Butter a large plate.

Bring the water to the boil with the salt, then add the maize flour little by little, stirring so that no lumps are formed. At first it will look very watery, but quite soon it will become thicker. Keep stirring. You might need to reduce the heat. Since all flours are slightly different, keep a little extra ready-boiled salty water on hand, to add in case the mixture becomes too stiff. After about 6 or 7 minutes, add a little butter and stir. Add the Parmesan and stir again for 2 or 3 minutes.

Turn the polenta on to the buttered plate. After a few minutes it will be quite solid and can be cut into slices for serving. Accompany it with some soft cheeses such as Gorgonzola or a mature Brie or with a porcini mushroom sauce.

This is the easy, 'modern' way to make polenta; however, for some, this is not as flavoursome as the more traditional method. For a more authentic result you can make it the traditional way with coarsely ground maize (*farina bramata*). This will involve a minimum of 50 minutes of constant stirring with a stick (*bastone*), unless you use the method suggested by Anna Del Conte, which she calls *senza bastone* (without a stick) or 'polenta made in the oven', and which I have used more than once. Rather than stirring energetically for a long time, you can simply stir the mixture for about five minutes, then cover the pan with baking paper and a tight-fitting lid, and put it in a cool oven (120–130°C, 250°F, gas mark 1 or 2) for about 35–40 minutes. Then you just turn it out on to a plate and, hey presto, a really tasty polenta without too much trouble.[68]

Sarah Bentham, a widow who worked as a guide in Italy, probably had polenta too as a traditional accompaniment to a meal she was served at an inn in Padua in 1792. It consisted of 'some excellent small birds roasted for dinner, which they called thrushes – and sheep brains fried in small pieces … sorrel generally made a side dish and meat pounded in a mortar and baked in a mould often appeared like a pudding and macaroni in a variety of forms.'[69]

One of my favourite visitors to Italy in the second half of the eighteenth century is the uplifting Mrs Piozzi, whom we have encountered earlier. She was married to a wealthy brewer, Mr Thrale, but after his death she fell in love with her daughter's music teacher, Gabriele Piozzi, and travelled with him through France, Italy and Germany.

While in Italy, in the summer of 1785, she tasted some very special local cherries in Florence, the 'bleeding-hearts, hard to bite and parting easily from the stone'. In terms of flavour, Mrs Piozzi wrote, they far exceeded the ones on sale in London though the latter were as big as plums. She also enjoyed figs 'small and green on the outside, a bright full crimson within' eaten with 'raw ham, and truly delicious'. The ham was most probably Tuscan, similar to but saltier than Parma ham. She also added that 'by raw ham, I mean ham cured, not boiled or roasted', indicating that this was still unusual in England.[70]

In her diary, she also enthused about a 'masquerade' with dancing in Naples, followed by a banquet prepared at one o'clock in the morning:

quite the finest supper of its size I ever saw. Fish of various sorts, incomparable in their kinds, composed eight dishes of the first course; we had thirty-eight set on the table in that course, forty-nine in the second, with wines and desserts truly magnificent.[71]

In the Neapolitan capital, they obviously knew how to enjoy themselves at table, and Mrs Piozzi had great fun in joining the party.

Apart from recording what she liked, and the atmosphere of the towns she preferred,[72] Mrs Piozzi also entertained 'many of the Tuscan, and many of the English nobility' at a dinner of her own, on 25 July 1785.[73] It is most likely that when she returned to England she gathered friends and acquaintances and contributed to spreading the knowledge and appreciation of all good things Italian, making them more than an enticing prospect. Some essential ingredients were already available through the Italian warehouses, and after her stint in Italy, this domestic goddess knew how to throw a great party. Her *Observations and Reflections Made in the Course of a Journey through France, Italy and Germany*, published in 1789, was read by George III's Queen Charlotte to her friend the satirical writer (and Keeper of Her Majesty's Robes) Frances Burney 'to their mutual delight'.[74] This must have certainly contributed to the book's popularity.

Margaret (which she later 'refined' to Marguerite) Gardiner, was an Irish beauty and a writer, who has also left a fascinating account of Italian travels with her second husband, the Earl of Blessington.[75] When she arrived in Genoa in March 1823, the first thing she did was to call on her idol, Lord Byron, who at the time lived near the city. For nearly three months, Margaret, her husband and Byron regularly met and had dinner together on a number of occasions.[76] Unfortunately nothing was ever mentioned about what they ate. However, the menus they were offered were probably based on French *haute cuisine*, and that most Genoese of basil sauces, *pesto*, was probably not part of any meal, on account of the presence of garlic. As Marguerite makes quite clear in her writings, her preference was for French cooking. In contrast, Byron celebrated humble pasta as the food of exotic love in *Don Juan*: 'Ceres presents a plate of vermicelli / for love must be sustain'd like flesh and blood.' (Canto II, stanza 170).

Lady Blessington's travelogue, *The Idler in Italy*, published in three volumes in 1839–40, had a considerable impact in England, because it was lively and well written, with a good deal of gossip and personal anecdotes.[77] For example, when she reached the north-east of Italy, she was rather disappointed with the standard of accommodation and food at Vicenza: 'Nowhere have I seen a worse inn, or streets so unclean, and crowded by a population more ill-looking'.[78] She asked her coach driver to find a better room 'or less disgusting looking food', and luckily he did in nearby Verona. There Lady Blessington had a completely different experience; the city was one of the most interesting she had ever seen – 'its cleanliness offers a very pleasing contrast to Vicenza'. The hotel was 'excellent' and the rooms had been occupied by 'His Majesty the Emperor of this, or the King of that; here slept the Prince so-and-so, or the Ambassador of —'. She commented that 'the *cuisine* too, of this hotel, is of a very superior description; for a dinner was served to us soon after our arrival, that would not have disparaged Lointies' [Lointier] at Paris. In short, the hotel, attendants and all, render an abode of some weeks at Verona not only agreeable but tempting.'[79]

Lady Blessington's books sold very well and she received an income of between £2,000 and £3,000 per annum (that's about £75,000–£80,000 in today's money), although this did not prevent her from getting into debt and fleeing to Paris, where she died aged sixty.

Advertisement for Mrs Holt's Italian warehouse c.1794. The etching, attributed to Hogarth, represents Mercury talking to a lady symbolizing Florence at whose feet there are a violin, a jar of olive oil, a hat and other items. In the distance there are men loading goods onto a ship and a view of Rome. The coat of arms of the Medici family and more views of Naples, Venice, Genoa and Livorno frame the vignette

two, then drained, and put in an oven dish with a pound of bone marrow distributed at the bottom of the dish, followed by a layer of vermicelli, until all the ingredients are finished. At this point Glasse instructs her readers to beat ten eggs (eggs were smaller in the eighteenth century), and add to them some breadcrumbs, one gill of brandy, salt, nutmeg, lemon zest, two blades of mace, currants and raisins, and bake for one and a half hours 'in an oven not too hot'. And just before serving, it can be topped with sugar, candied orange peel and citron.[87]

The 'vermicella' pudding could be followed by a 'Shoulder of Veal à la Piemontoise', a well-seasoned joint of meat with lots of herbs including pepper, mace, sweet herbs, parsley and so on. The final result is a kind of stew, to which 'The French strew it over with Parmesan before it goes to the oven.'[88] For dessert, Glasse suggests an 'Italian Pudding' made with cream, bread, eggs, red wine, and puff pastry, all baked for one hour.[89] And there you have it: an Italian supper, eighteenth-century British style.

Italian food was gaining fame, and not just in Britain. On the other side of the Atlantic, Thomas Jefferson, the principal author of the American Declaration of Independence and third president of the United States, was among the champions of Italian cuisine.

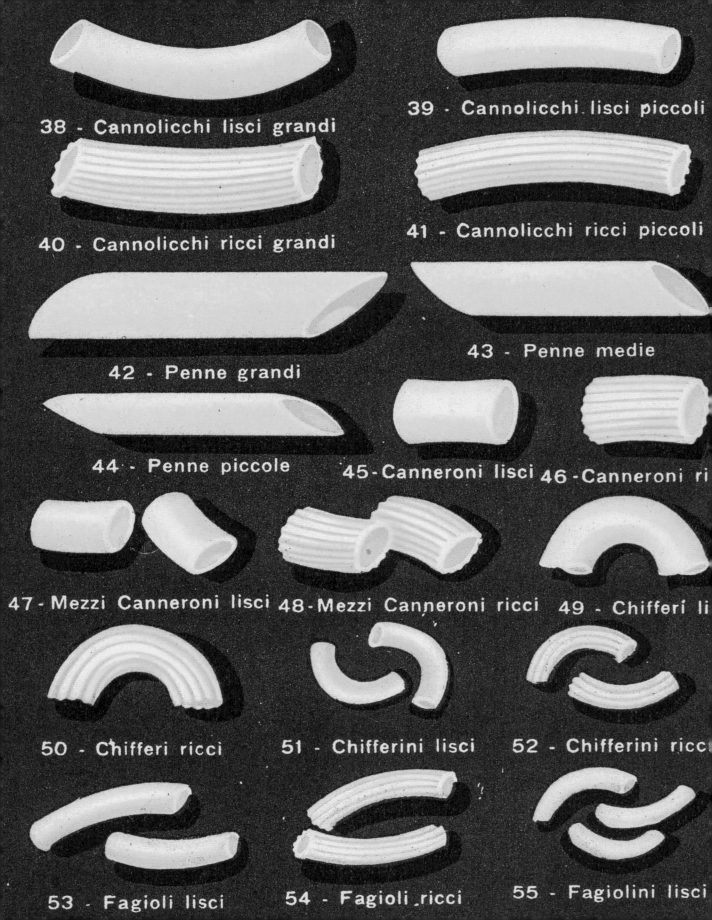

38 - Cannolicchi lisci grandi

39 - Cannolicchi lisci piccoli

40 - Cannolicchi ricci grandi

41 - Cannolicchi ricci piccoli

42 - Penne grandi

43 - Penne medie

44 - Penne piccole

45 - Canneroni lisci

46 - Canneroni ri

47 - Mezzi Canneroni lisci

48 - Mezzi Canneroni ricci

49 - Chifferi li

50 - Chifferi ricci

51 - Chifferini lisci

52 - Chifferini ricc

53 - Fagioli lisci

54 - Fagioli ricci

55 - Fagiolini lisci

4. THEY CALL IT MACARONI

AT THE END OF THE EIGHTEENTH CENTURY, Italy was still the land of the Grand Tour and the ultimate destination for affluent British visitors. Apart from works of art and ancient monuments, some travellers were also intrigued by the food served in inns and taverns, at private functions or simply sold in the streets. A deep curiosity for things Italian had also started on the other side of the Atlantic, and long before Italian immigrants landed at Staten Island.

AMERICANS IN PARIS (AND ITALY)

When Thomas Jefferson was posted to Europe in 1784 he followed in the footsteps of his compatriot Benjamin Franklin, who had been living in France for nearly twenty years and was at the time the fledgling United States's first ambassador to the country. Despite having declared in his *Autobiography* that he had no interest in food, Franklin was known as a great organizer of sumptuous dinners in the French capital.[1] And it was there that Jefferson tasted a delicious dish by the name of *macaroni*. He enjoyed it so much that he decided to find out more about it. However, on his quest he was first sidetracked by another ingredient: the Parmesan grated on top. Where did the cheese come from? And how was it produced? To satisfy his curiosity, Jefferson spent a whole day in Rozzano, near Milan, at a dairy farm where he learnt the intricacies of Parmesan production.

Freshly produced cow's milk was collected in the evening and put in large vats to which some of the milk from the morning's milking was added. The milk was then partially skimmed over a period of eight to ten hours. The skimmed milk was poured into the cheese-making cauldrons, usually made of copper, to which a small quantity of whey left over from the previous cheese-making cycle was added. The milk was then slowly heated and when it reached a lukewarm temperature rennet was added, which caused curds to form. The curd was then broken and stirred, producing typical granules, which were further cooked to a higher temperature. The granules settled to the bottom of the cauldrons and whey was then removed. The soft mass of granules was at this point transferred into suspended linen cloths to remove some more moisture and when ready put into special round moulds. After a couple of days, the cheese was treated with brine for a fortnight or up to a month. The salt removed even more moisture and helped the formation of the rind. The cheese was left to mature for at least a year, but it would reach its best after two years. Jefferson was also most likely to have been told that there were two seasonal varieties of Parmesan: the one produced in the summer, when pastures were green, was tastier and of a more intense yellow than the winter variety, when cows were fed on hay or other dry fodder.

Cheese was not Jefferson's only diversion. He knew that nearby Piedmont was becoming famed for its rice production. Although the word *risotto* had not been coined yet,[2] various types of *minestra* (soup) made with boiled rice and butter, or vegetables, were widely available, especially in Turin.[3] So he acquired a horse and proceeded to inspect a farm in the countryside. Although it was strictly forbidden to remove rice in the husk and export it, a crime punishable by death, Jefferson chanced it and put a handful of seeds into his pockets. With the help of a local muleteer, who procured him a bigger quantity of rice, he smuggled it to the port of Genoa.

Jefferson's motives and intentions were purely scientific. He sent the Italian rice to the South Carolina Society for Promoting Agriculture to establish whether it was better than the American variety. Eventually the local scientists found that American rice was preferable for their purposes.[4] Evidently the Italian types of rice were suitable for local dishes but quite different from long American grains.

During his four-year stay in Europe, Jefferson was keen to learn as much as he could about agricultural techniques, animal husbandry and the growing of

94

Monticello, Virginia: home to Thomas Jefferson, who ordered Italian peaches, apricots and grapes to be grown nearby

fruit trees, vines and vegetables. He had studied Latin authors on agriculture, including the works of Cato and Varro, and considered modern Italians as the heirs of the classical tradition. Through a mutual friend, he made contact with Filippo Mazzei, a Tuscan surgeon, teacher and importer of wine and other Italian goods in London, and persuaded this extraordinary character to join him in Virginia for a special venture.[5]

Filippo, or Philip as he later became known, wasted no time and accepted Jefferson's proposal. In September 1773 Mazzei boarded ship at Livorno together with a young tailor, a few farmers from Tuscany, the widow of a friend and her daughter, and numerous plants and seeds. As soon as the party landed that November, Mazzei and his men were put in charge of planting

Italian peaches, apricots and grapes near Monticello, Jefferson's property. Jefferson persuaded Mazzei to purchase some land that Mazzei renamed Il Colle, 'the hill', in honour of his beloved Tuscany.[6]

At first the agricultural experiments were not a success, but later it was recognized that Mazzei's contribution to the cultivation of vines and olives was of great importance and the Tuscan doctor received the gratitude of 'a great portion' of the American States and of Jefferson himself.[7] In all of this, he had also been active in politics and participated in the revolutionary war against the British.

AT THE WHITE HOUSE

While still in France, in 1787 Jefferson drew up plans for a pasta-making machine (illustrated on page 97), and I believe he may even have conceived the idea of producing pasta in Virginia or Pennsylvania. Two years later he was back in Washington, and in 1801 he became the third President of the United States. It was then that he asked his friends in France to send him a quantity of macaroni, Parmesan cheese, figs and anchovies. As president, he enjoyed entertaining on a grand scale. He had his cook, James, trained in the art of French cookery, while he himself improved his knowledge of Burgundy and other wines.[8] However, he enjoyed macaroni and Parmesan so much that at some of his official banquets he served nothing else.

One of his guests, Manasseh Cutler, a congressman from Massachusetts, jotted down his impression of a presidential dinner, which was not to his liking. The dinner consisted of:

> rice soup, round of beef, turkey, mutton, ham, loin of veal, cutlets of mutton, fried eggs, fried beef, and a pie called macaroni which appeared to be a rich brown crust ... a great variety of fruit, plenty of wines and good; ice-cream very good.[9]

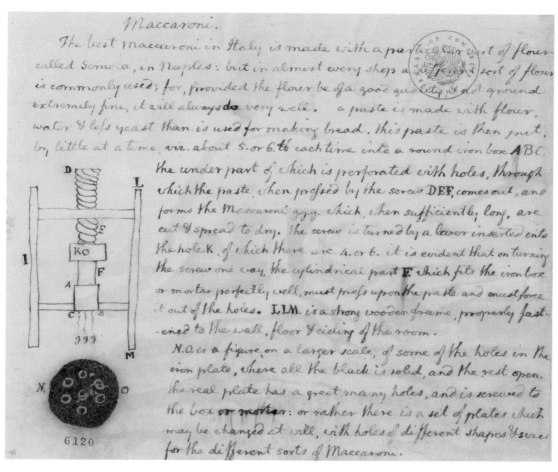

Thomas Jefferson's Maccaroni Recipe and Press Design c.1798. His holographic drawing for this contraption, with personal notes, has survived in the Library of Congress Washington, D.C., Manuscript Division, 1787.

Cutler had never tasted macaroni before; he thought it was some kind of onion, and did not enjoy it. From the crust in his description it was probably one of the first examples of 'mac and cheese'. There appeared in the 1824 edition of one of the most influential cookbooks of America, *The Virginia Housewife, or Methodical Cook*, written by a cousin of Thomas Jefferson's, with just such a recipe for macaroni. After boiling in milk and water the pasta is dressed with cheese and butter and baked in a 'quick oven'.[10]

In Philadelphia, a Frenchman had opened a pasta factory in 1798, and it seems to have been a successful enterprise, although upper-class Americans preferred to import their pasta directly from Sicily. But by the 1880s, macaroni recipes were published in numerous cookery books even in the remoter parts of America, including Kansas.

TASTING ITALIAN FOOD

How did other prominent American figures react to the type of catering they found in Italy in the first half of the nineteenth century? In this regard, we are fairly well informed, since most of them published books about their experiences, or at least kept diaries during their visits. What did they enjoy (or not)?

Tourism was still in its infancy, even in the major cities, and not many travellers were yet prepared to experiment with the foreignness of food. Chicken and pork were familiar, and many comment on the revelation of fresh figs, but although some realized that the discovery of new things had potentially an intrinsic value, others were simply in fear of finding something that did not fit with their ideas of 'a good meal'. Inevitably, some were attracted by the unknown, the novelty of it all, while others were positively deterred by it.

The author of *The Last of the Mohicans*, James Fenimore Cooper, visited Italy in 1838. While travelling in the Apennines, he found a satisfactory inn where he and his family, though worried about the possibility of being assaulted by *banditti*, stopped for supper, and 'ate chicken fried in oil undisturbed'. This is still a dish that one finds especially in Tuscany, and it is simply known as *pollo fritto*, small pieces of chicken fried in good olive oil.[11] Fenimore Cooper mentioned this dish again in his diary the next day, adding that the chicken, 'though saturated with oil, savoured more of Italy, and was so much more agreeable than the lame imitations of French cookery we had met with previously'.[12] This is a very appreciative remark that shows a desire, unlike many other foreign travellers of the time, to discover the real flavour of Italy and an awareness of what is genuine and what is not, even if he considered the amount of oil excessive.[13] It was, at least, 'good olive oil', and he was prepared to accept the use of a basic vegetable fat so different from the pork fat, butter or suet to which he was accustomed.

On reaching Tuscany, Fenimore Cooper remarked on the olive being 'a formal, insignificant tree in a landscape' but a plant that could still be looked at with pleasure, 'as one does also at the orange, the pomegranate, the fig, the date, and other trees of Oriental associations, though none but the fig has much beauty'.[14] The landscape and the food of Italy carried some aesthetic value for most travellers, but the fig had a particular significance for the American writer. Somewhere in central Italy a humble priest had taught him that eating a fig after soup was a delicious practice. So Fenimore Cooper decided to adopt it. He confirmed that this represented for him 'the very perfection of epicurism, or rather of taste, in the matter of eating. A single fresh fig, as a corrective after the soup, I hold to be one of those sublime touches of art, that are oftener discovered by accident than by the investigation of knowledge.'[15] The French had an equivalent practice, but he believed it did not compare: 'At Paris you are always offered a glass of Madeira after the soup, the only one taken at table, but it is a pitiful substitute for the fig.' In Naples he enthused about the one fig he enjoyed after his soup every day, defining it 'the luscious little green fellow, with a blood-red interior'.[16] Indeed an object of beauty and taste.

While travelling through Umbria with his family, another American author, Nathaniel Hawthorne, enjoyed in Terni 'for lunch an omelette, some stewed veal, and a dessert of figs and grapes, besides two decanters of a light-colored acid wine, tasting very like indifferent cider'.[17] A simple meal, which apart from the poor wine, must have given a positive impression to the family. And in Foligno they had 'a very fair and well-cooked dinner', which showed, according to Hawthorne, 'that it is still possible to live well, in Italy, at no great expense'.

When they reached Florence, on Monday 7 June 1858, they were visited in the evening by Hiram Powers, a well-known American sculptor of the era, who talked 'to begin with about Italian food, as poultry, mutton, beef,

and their lack of savoriness as compared with our own; and mentioned an exquisite dish of vegetables which they prepare from squash or pumpkin-blossoms'.[18]

This must be one of the earliest mentions in English of a popular Italian dish that goes back to at least the end of the eighteenth century.[19] The flowers of the pumpkin (*zucca*) or its relation courgette (*zucchini*) are still widely used, and are usually fried in a kind of Florentine tempura batter but can also be served with various fillings.

FIORI DI ZUCCA FRITTI

Serves 4–6

20 pumpkin (or courgette) flowers
10 anchovy fillets
sufficient olive oil to fry the flowers, at least 100ml (4 fl oz)

For the batter
2 medium eggs
1 tbsp olive oil
100g (4oz) wheat flour
good pinch of salt

Remove the delicate bitter orange stamen from inside each flower and check they are clean. If you need to rinse them, ensure they are thoroughly dry before cooking. Place half an anchovy fillet into each flower.

Prepare the batter by mixing the eggs with the oil, and slowly adding the flour and salt. You should get a fairly soft batter. Dip each flower in the batter, until it is covered. In a frying pan heat the oil to about 140–150°C (275–300°F), being careful not to reach smoking point. Throw the flowers into the pan, and carefully turn them. In a few moments the batter will turn golden and you can remove the flowers, one by one, with a slotted spoon, and arrange them on a plate with absorbent paper. Serve hot.

Powers also mentioned another dish, related to the previous one, that impressed Hawthorne for its novelty and potential, as something that he hoped to import to America:

> ... it will be well for us to remember when we get back at Wayside [their home in Concord, Massachusetts], where we are overrun with acacias. It consists of the acacia-blossom. In a certain stage of its development, fried in oil. I shall get the recipe from Mrs Powers, and mean to deserve well of my country by first trying it and then making it known; only I doubt whether American lard, or even butter, will produce the dish quite so deliciously as Florentine oil. [20]

Hawthorne's opinion of good olive oil seems more liberal than that of Fenimore Cooper and others, but his notebook shows that this type of oil was still very rare or unobtainable in America. (It is interesting to note that 'oilmen' and Italian warehousemen in nineteenth-century England usually stored all or some of the following oils: 'Fine Lucca, Florence, Genoa', plus linseed and other oils for lamps or perfume, such as spermaceti.)[21] Among America's affluent urbanites, foraging for wild flowers might also have been viewed with suspicion, but in Italy, flower fritters had been included in recipe books for the aristocracy since the Renaissance, especially elderflowers eaten with a sprinkling of sugar.[22]

In October the Hawthorne family was still in Tuscany, first in Radicofani, near Siena, and then in nearby San Quirico d'Orcia, nowadays one of the most photographed villages in Tuscany.[23] There they enjoyed a *déjeuner à la fourchette*, and in the best tavern, the Aquila Nera (which Hawthorne calls 'The Eagle'), they were served 'an omelette, some boiled beef, a couple of roast chickens, grapes, and roasted chickens [sic] with abundance of thin red wine', a very satisfactory meal. In this description, as well as the lack of vegetables, there is no mention of soup, but the omelette probably substituted as a first course.[24]

Adriaen Coort, *Three Peaches on a Stone Plinth*, oil on panel, 1705

When it comes to beverages, Hawthorne was intrigued by the old system of producing wine must by crushing the grapes 'with a sort of pestle' or, even more, using unwashed peasants' feet: 'It is a shame to turn such delicious juice into such sour wine as they make in Tuscany!' He hoped to find the juice similar to a 'nectar' he had sampled as a child in America, that of 'new cider, which I used to suck with a straw in my boyhood', but the result of this wine-tasting was quite disastrous: 'Positively, I never tasted anything so detestable – such a sour and bitter juice, still lukewarm with fermentation; it was a wail of a woe, squeezed out of the wine press of tribulation, and the more a man drinks of such the sorrier he will be.'

Not a good advertisement for Tuscan wines, but their current high quality was only developed years later, in particular thanks to Baron Bettino Ricasoli, who succeeded with the first Chianti in 1872, after many years of research and experiments. It is interesting that Hawthorne, while comparing the cider-making of New England, which he found far more picturesque than an Italian vintage, added an essentially aesthetic remark: 'Nothing connected with the grape culture and the vintage is picturesque, except the huge inverted pyramids in which the clusters hang; those great bunches, white or purple, really satisfy my idea both as to aspect and taste.'[25]

Overall, the food Hawthorne experienced did not fit his own romantic or picturesque view of Italian life and history. It proved too linked with the poverty that he saw around him and described so vividly. He did not seem to have found anything representing the kind of refined high cuisine that he had encountered in France. After all, a certain widespread affluence is needed to appreciate rustic dishes. The majority of the establishments he visited were rather pedestrian, but Hawthorne seemed fully aware that in some cases the experience of English and American travellers had already contributed to improving the general standard of food provision along the most popular touring routes.

At this time Italy was still a conglomerate of discrete small states. Strong regional differences, sometimes difficult to understand and even more to appreciate, were widespread, and still are.

Back in Rome, in March 1859, Hawthorne gave a lively account of the sudden appearance of a 'fritter establishment' in the piazza where they lived at the time. It was equipped with a kind of cauldron where the owners started frying large quantities of 'simply dough, cut into squares or rhomboids'. Having tried one of the strange fritters he found that 'it resembled an unspeakably bad doughnut, without any sweetening. In fact it was sour, for the Romans like their bread, and all their preparations of flour, in a state of acetous fermentation, which serves them instead of salt or other condiment.'[26] This is a good example of a street food that is enjoyed by the locals but incomprehensible to the foreign visitor. The fritter shop, which had sprung up overnight, stayed for one weekend only. On Monday morning it had already disappeared. The mention of the acid fermentation of bread may be a reference to an early type of sourdough, but to appreciate it one should have been acquainted with a multiplicity of dishes based on different types of pasta.

What Hawthorne had experienced were traditional fritters made mainly during Carnival, even if, as he says, it was 'Friday, and Lent besides'. They were known by a variety of local and regional names such as *bugie* (Piedmont), *cenci* (Tuscany), *fràppole* (Veneto) and produced in many parts of Italy. Sometimes they would be sprinkled with vanilla and sugar, or at least that is how they were made in my own region when I was a child. They may belong to an ancient tradition that goes back to the *frictilia* made in ancient Rome for special early spring festivals. I once made them for a party with my students, and they were a great success and devoured in great quantity, regardless of Hawthorne's opinion.

FESTIVE FRITTERS

Serves 5–6

3 large eggs, plus one yolk

500g (1lb) wheat flour (preferably Italian 00 grade)

1 tsp baking powder

good pinch of salt

120g (4–5oz) caster sugar

2 tbsp liquor (grappa, rum or brandy)

seeds scraped from 1 vanilla pod

50g (2oz) butter at room temperature

about 200ml (7 fl oz) groundnut or sunflower oil, for frying

Beat the eggs, and then sift the flour into a separate bowl together with the baking powder. Add salt, sugar, liquor, vanilla seeds, soft butter and the previously beaten eggs. Knead the mixture carefully by hand or in a pasta mixer, for at least 10 minutes.

Once you have a smooth, supple dough (you may need to add a drop of water if the dough is too crumbly), make a ball, cover with kitchen film and leave to rest for about half an hour. At this stage you will need a pasta machine, unless you are very skilled with a rolling pin. Take approximately 100g (4oz) of the dough, flatten it slightly by pressing it with your hand, and pass it through the pasta machine rolls, starting with the larger setting, then progressing to a medium setting (approximately 2mm or 1/8in).

Lay the sheet of pasta on a floured surface and cut it into rectangles, rhomboids or narrower strips, preferably with a wheel that gives a decorative edge. Repeat until you have pressed and cut all the dough.

Heat the vegetable oil to approximately 140–150°C (275–300°F), then add the squares or strips of pasta, a few at a time, to the pan, splashing them with oil so that the top of each fritter turns a nice delicate golden hue. Turn the fritters with a spoon and check the colour; after a few minutes you can remove them with a slotted spoon and leave them on absorbent paper to cool, when you can sprinkle them with icing sugar. The fritters have a festive appearance and go well with dessert wines, such as Vin Santo, Torcolato, Barsac, Monbazillac, or even some sparkling demi-sec.

MACARONI FOR ALL

Fenimore Cooper provides us with a few more details about what was available in Italy in the early part of the nineteenth century. While travelling in the north in 1838, he visited a food market in Lodi, near Milan, where he spotted a neat row of what, from a distance, looked like small white birds on display. As he got nearer, he realized that they were actually 'the hind quarters of frogs', and he added that Italians, contrary to a popular belief but confirming what earlier British travellers had noticed, eat more frogs than the French, especially in Lombardy.[27] Nowadays frogs are no longer very popular, partly because their natural habitats of swamps and small ponds have been destroyed, and partly because the figure of the frog-fisher, still active until the 1950s, has now completely disappeared.[28]

Fenimore Cooper also remarked that Parmesan was an important ingredient, not only in Lombardy, but all over Italy, and that a tablespoon of the grated cheese was obligatory on soup, as Coryat and Skippon had noticed nearly two hundred years before.[29] This seems to indicate that culinary practices were unchanging over long periods of time. And this brings us back to macaroni. When talking about the crowds he observed in the streets of Naples, Fenimore Cooper compared them to the groups of people who would gather 'around a kettle of macaroni ... were its contents declared free'.[30] The Italian dish, with its connotations of cheapness and easy fulfilment, was in common use in America by now. Hawthorne mentioned it in a page of his *American Notebooks*, when, during his wife's absence for about three weeks one summer, he was in charge of his five-year-old son Julian and his pet rabbit. The child complained of stomach ache in the morning but later in the day 'he ate a good dinner of maccaroni, rice, squash and bread'.[31] The combination of macaroni and rice may seem a little strange, but it was obviously appreciated by young Julian. It represented a simple, nutritious, and effective type of comfort food. (In 1959 Vincent De Domenico, a pasta maker from San Francisco, created a commercial concoction called Rice-a-

John Singer Sargent, *Breakfast in the Loggia*, oil on canvas, 1910

Roni after watching his sister-in-law mixing vermicelli and rice with canned chicken broth.)[32]

We also have evidence of macaroni sold by grocers in London, and that this dish and 'timbale de macaroni' appeared on menus for formal dinners in London for most of the nineteenth century. The critic, essayist and poet Leigh Hunt made some detailed remarks on the importance of soup, or rather *minestra*, and macaroni that are worth quoting in full:

> If Italy is famous at present for any two things, it is for political uneasiness [he must have been there during the unrest of 1831] and *minestra*. Wherever you find shops, you see baskets full of a yellow stuff, made up in long stripes like tape, and tied up in bundles. This is the main compound of *minestra*, or, to use the Neapolitan term, it is our now growing acquaintance *maccaroni*. Much of it is naturally of a yellowish colour, but the Genoese dye it deeper with saffron. When made into a soup it is called *minestra*, and mixed sometimes with meat, sometimes with oil, sometimes with oil or butter, but always, if it is to be had, with grated cheese.[33]

Leigh Hunt recognized that macaroni was becoming a new feature of catering in Britain, a fact borne out in John Mollard's *The Art of Cookery* (1801).[34] Mollard was a chef at the London Tavern in Bishopsgate and later in the Freemason's Tavern in Great Queen Street. His book included some interesting recipes inspired by Italian cooking, such as a 'Genoese soup', a vermicelli soup (white), macaroni and Parmesan cheese soup, fillet of mutton à l'italienne, to be served with an Italian sauce, and a 'Pupton of chicken, rabbits etc'. Pupton in the *OED* is defined as 'a baked dish made with meat or fruit', and the rare gastronomic term may have come, via the French *poupton*, from Italian *polpettone*.

Eliza Acton, a poet as well as a celebrated cook, was the first to use the word *spaghetti* in the English language. In her influential *Modern Cookery for Private Families* (1845), she explained the differences between Naples macaroni 'of which the pipes are large' and the ones from Genoa, smaller in size but more substantial, probably meaning thicker.[35] The Genoese, she advised, are

Timbales of macaroni from Charles Francatelli, *The Modern Cook*, 1846

better suited 'for the formation of the fanciful timbales, for which it is usually chosen'. She does not give a recipe for such timbales, because of the difficulty involved in their preparation, but a whole section devoted to timbales (*timballi*) can be found in a classic Italian recipe book of 1773, *Il cuoco galante* (*The Refined Cook*) by the Neapolitan monk Vincenzo Corrado. He starts by pointing out the similarity between pies and timbales, as both compound dishes, but then describes a typical *timballo*. Most would be made with short lengths of cooked macaroni stirred into a fatty beef and pork sauce, enclosed in a pastry case and layered with a ragout of sausages, sweetbreads and ham. Sometimes mozzarella and Parmesan would be added before baking the timbale in the oven.[36] In his novel *The Leopard* the Sicilian writer Giuseppe Tomasi di Lampedusa (1896–1957) describes a sumptuous dinner where a majestic timbale of macaroni is given centre stage.[37] In the eponymous film directed by Luchino Visconti in 1963, the scene is made unforgettable. This is my version, loosely based on various ancient recipes.

TIMBALLO DI MACCHERONI

Serves 6–8

2 tbsp olive oil

50g (2oz) pancetta or streaky bacon, minced

1 shallot or small onion, chopped

1 small carrot, finely chopped

1 small stick celery, chopped

Half a clove of garlic, peeled and chopped

500g (1lb) beef, minced

100ml (4 fl oz) red wine

800g (1¾lb) tinned tomatoes

good pinch marjoram

bay leaf

salt and pepper

grated nutmeg

20g (1oz) butter

50g (2oz) dried porcini mushrooms, soaked in warm water for about 20 minutes, then rinsed and squeezed. If large, chop into pieces

200g (8oz) chicken livers, diced. For those who dislike liver, an equivalent weight of cooked ham, roughly chopped, will do as well

50g (2oz) giblets, diced (some spicy salami, roughly chopped, can be substituted)

2 sheets shortcrust pastry (about 215g or 7–8oz each)

2 hardboiled eggs, sliced. Or quail eggs (at least 6) work very well

500g (1lb) pasta: *sedani*, short macaroni or *penne rigate*

100g (4oz) Parmesan, freshly grated

1 fresh mozzarella (about 150g or 5oz), sliced in small strips

100g (4oz) ricotta

First prepare the sauce by gently frying the pancetta, onion, carrot and celery in the olive oil. After about 5 minutes, add the garlic, continue to fry for another 2–3 minutes, then add the minced meat small spoonfuls at a time. Make sure that it is frying but on a low heat. Stir frequently. Once the meat is caramelized slightly – this may take up to 20 minutes – add the wine and, when almost all evaporated, the tomatoes, marjoram, bay leaf, salt and pepper. Cover the pan, and simmer slowly for another 30 or 40 minutes.

Add most of the butter (reserve a little for greasing the timbale dish later), porcini, chicken livers and giblets (or chopped ham and salami), and simmer for another 20 minutes or so. If the sauce seems too dry add some hot water, and stir. Remove the bay leaf and leave to cool.

Heat the oven to 160°C (325°F).

Boil the pasta in a large pan of salted water until it is just cooked, but still firm (say one minute less than the time stated on the packet). Drain, and mix well with the tomato and meat sauce. Sprinkle some grated nutmeg (about half a teaspoon) over the pasta. Stir in half the Parmesan.

Assemble the timbale. Thoroughly grease the sides of a large ovenproof dish (at least 25cm or 10in in diameter) with a little butter, line the sides and the base with the pastry, and reserve a piece sufficient to cover the top of your dish, which will become the base of the timbale. Instead of pastry as a wrapper I have sometimes used long thin slices of aubergines fried in good olive oil.

Put a layer of macaroni and sauce in the bottom, top with a few pieces of mozzarella, a little ricotta and slices of hard-boiled eggs, and continue to build up layers until all the ingredients have been used up. Cover with the disc of pastry, and bake for about 30 minutes. Remove and leave to cool slightly. Turn the timbale onto a serving plate, cut into slices to serve, and add the rest of the Parmesan to each plate.

DICKENS IN ITALY

In some of his work, the great English writer Charles Dickens liked to describe the difficulties of travellers pressed for time at the 'refreshment' places in the newly created railway stations. In his short story 'Refreshments for Travellers', he gave various humorous accounts of food that was not up to scratch: 'I find that I must either scald my throat by insanely ladling into it, against time and for no wager, brown hot water stiffened with flour' or digging out of some very hard pastry 'some glutinous lumps of gristle and grease, called pork-pie'.[38] Incompetent or simply obnoxious waiters are also part of the scene. All this seems to bear a certain similarity to his description of food in Italy.

Dickens' interest in food comes through in the accounts of his numerous travels abroad. In his *Pictures from Italy*, deriving from his visit in 1845, he gives us a brief account of three different meals: the first one in 'a real Genoese tavern', the second while travelling northwards from Genoa, the third near Siena. In Genoa he had some taglierini, though he did not tell us what it was served with. It could have been a soup, or *minestra*. But in Genoa it could have been accompanied by pesto, which is now exclusively associated with basil, but in the past could include various herbs crushed in a mortar.[39] Another typical Genoese dish, according to him, was ravioli, and I suspect these were served with sage butter and Parmesan. Then 'German sausages, strong of garlic, sliced and eaten with fresh green figs'. This is the most intriguing entry. What the writer ate was probably a garlic salami from the area north of Genoa that reminded him of some German sausages. Other items on the menu seemed more complicated, even fanciful: 'cock's combs and sheep-kidneys, chopped up with mutton chops and liver; small pieces of some unknown part of a calf, twisted into small shreds, and served up in a great dish like whitebait and other curiosities of that kind'.[40] Other visitors to Italy had remarked on the fact that cock's combs were sold by butchers, and were obviously popular. But the dish as a whole sounds like a stew or possibly

Luis Melendez, *Still Life with Figs and Bread*, oil on canvas, c.1770

Timbales of macaroni from Charles Francatelli, *The Modern Cook*, 1846

a fricassee, containing something like sweetbreads, and possibly some tripe (those unidentifiable twists of small shreds).

On his way to Parma at the beginning of November, Dickens depicts the journey and his fellow travellers: the passage is a little masterpiece of realism and humour. I was rather interested in this part of his trip because he mentioned that he was 'bound for a good many places (England among them), but first for Piacenza'. However, in the middle of the night, in cold, unpleasant weather, they stopped at Stradella, a small place I remember well because my father used to buy wine there. Towards midnight, the few passengers were taken to some 'immensely broad deal dining-tables', and eventually supper was served: 'The first dish is a cabbage, boiled with a great quantity of rice in a tureen full of water, and flavoured with cheese. It is so hot, and we are so cold, that it appears almost jolly.' The second dish consisted of 'some little bits of pork, fried with pig's kidneys'. The third, two red fowls, probably partridges, the fourth, two little turkeys, which could also be guinea fowl. The fifth, a 'huge stew of garlic and truffle, and I don't know what else'.[41]

How far back can we find the recipes for some of these dishes? The first one seems to me a traditional winter dish from Lombardy, known locally as *riso e verze*, rice with Savoy cabbage, eaten as a hearty soup. A variant of this was used to celebrate the last day of the preparation and salting of a home-bred pig.

116

RISO E VERZE

Serves 4–6

30g butter

1 tbsp extra virgin olive oil

1 onion, finely chopped

1 celery stick, finely chopped

300g (10–12oz) green Savoy cabbage, finely cut and chopped

150g (5oz) lean pork, minced

50g (2oz) *pancetta* or streaky bacon, minced

½ tsp ground cinnamon

½ tsp ground nutmeg

1 tbsp red wine

1 small clove garlic, finely chopped

salt and pepper

500ml (1pt) stock (chicken, or beef and pork)

500ml (1pt) water

40–50g (1½–2oz) rice per person, preferably Vialone or Arborio

In a large pan heat the butter and oil. Add the chopped onion, celery and cabbage. Turn the mixture for about 5 minutes.

Mix the minced meats with the cinnamon, nutmeg, red wine, garlic and salt and pepper, and add it to the pan. Keep turning on a moderate heat until the pork and *pancetta* are melting and lightly brown (about 7–8 minutes).

Bring the stock and water to the boil, add to the pan of meat and vegetables, cover and simmer for at least half an hour. If necessary add more stock or water.

When almost ready to serve, add the rice, turning with a spoon. After approximately 18–20 minutes the rice should be ready. Taste, correct seasoning if necessary, and serve. A good wine like Barbera from Asti, or a Dolcetto or Chianti, would be an excellent accompaniment.

The second dish Dickens describes is obviously kidneys sautéed with lardons (the 'little bits of pork'), which is something mentioned in English establishments, as well as in his fiction. The final course he mentions, the stew of truffles, is puzzling, and the presence of garlic makes me suspicious, since, as far as I know, it is never used with real truffles. Given the season, could they have been Jerusalem artichokes? There is evidence that these tubers were referred to as 'white truffles' in Italy as early as 1738.[42] Maybe something got lost in translation.

Later, we find Dickens in bleak country somewhere south of Siena, at an *osteria* called La Scala:

> We had the usual dinner in this solitary house; and a very good dinner it is, when you are used to it. There is something with a vegetable or some rice in it, which is a sort of shorthand or arbitrary character for soup, and which tastes very well, when you have flavoured it with plenty of grated cheese, lots of salt, and an abundance of pepper.'[43]

He goes on to mention 'half fowl of which this soup has been made. There is a stewed pigeon with the gizzards and livers of himself and other birds stuck all around it.' It is obvious that offal, and especially fowl entrails, were much more common than today. After the pigeon comes 'a bit of roast beef, the size of a small French roll'. If it were a prime piece of beef, it would have been expensive, and therefore rather small, but to someone used to 'joints ready for the spits' and the renowned roast beef of England, it may have looked even more insignificant. After the roast, which he obviously found unsatisfactory, he mentions by way of a dessert 'a scrap of Parmesan cheese, and five little withered apples, all huddled together on a small plate, and crowding one upon the other, as if each were trying to save itself from the chance of being eaten. Then there is coffee.'[44] And then, one finally goes to bed.

To sum up, most travellers to Italy at this time mention some kind of soup, either with rice and vegetables or served as a *minestra*, with its variant of pasta

Ulisse Aldrovandi, Squash vine, late 16th century

Joseph Decker, *Grapes*, oil on canvas, c.1890–95

5. ITALIAN FOOD IN LONDON

WAS IT FRENCH? WAS IT ITALIAN? It was a treat that everybody could afford, and in the summer it sold, well, better than hot cakes. Ice-cream may have been an exclusive invention of sixteenth-century royal courts,[1] but in Victorian times it reached all levels of society in London and in Scotland, thanks to the hard work of Italian immigrants.[2] When the very first ice-creams were sold in England, people did not always know how to react, and contemporary journalists and cartoonists remarked on the strange and even disturbing, cold feeling on the tongue. Henry Mayhew, in his massive *London Labour and the London Poor* (1861–2) reported that the buyers had a confused notion of how the ice was to be swallowed, and one street dealer explained that he had 'seen the people splutter when they've tasted them [the ice-creams] for the first time! ... They get among the teeth and make you feel as if you tooth-ached all over.'[3]

However, this novelty soon became very popular. At first ices, or penny licks, as they were also known, were sold from handheld barrows, and the vendors, who were often Italian, were sometimes called the 'hokey pokey men'. This curious name may have evolved from an Italian phrase uttered by the sellers, such as '*Ecco un poco*', 'Here's a little', possibly referring to the low cost of the ice-cream. Later, more elaborate vans took the place of the hokey pokey men, some of them decorated by the owners themselves; their motorized descendants still reveal their presence with their typical 'ice-cream jingle' all children recognize.[4]

London in the 1840s was expanding and attracting large numbers of immigrants, many of whom came from various Italian states.[5] A few of them were skilled artisans, but the majority made a living by working as waiters in the expanding cafés and hotels, or as domestic servants. Many made ends meet by costermongering, that is selling fruit, such as oranges and apples, in the streets, or begging while grinding out music from a handheld organ.[6] But when ice-creams became a kind of fashion, a large number of London Italians, mainly living in Clerkenwell, Holborn, Saffron Hill and Soho, could be seen setting out around 4 a.m. to get the necessary milk and sugar to start the icing process. By around 7.30 they were ready to sell their penny ices. It was a hard life, but for some lucky ones there were reasonable returns. By 1880, Italians controlled the ice-cream market, and by the end of the century there were about 900 ice-cream barrows based in London's Little Italy alone.[7] In time some well-organized ice-cream vendors started controlling other sellers and acquiring large quantities of ice to expand their business.

Carlo Gatti from Italian Switzerland was one such. He arrived in London in 1847, aged thirty, after a short period in France, and made a living by selling chestnuts and chocolate, before dedicating himself to ice-cream production.[8] He was lucky enough to marry a girl whose father owned two cafés in London. Carlo obviously had an entrepreneurial spirit and came up with a bright idea: why not get ice from where it's cheaper? He managed to make contact with someone in Norway who would ship huge quantities at a lower cost. He had an ice-well, and then another, built near the docks.[9] This allowed him and the vendors that depended on him to produce large quantities of ice-cream, and to expand the sales of the two family shops. He later turned some of the catering premises into music halls, and became known as one of the top entertainers in London.

Obviously, not all the local inhabitants were happy with the large numbers of penny-ice men. In fact, there were attempts to reduce the activities of the Italians on the grounds that their ingredients or their methods of production were unhygienic, even poisonous, according to unproven accusations at the time. Essentially, ice-cream is just sweetened and flavoured cow's milk brought to below freezing temperature by being stirred in a metal container surrounded by a freezing mixture (usually ice). The recipe for plain ice-cream, such as this one from 1881, was quite simple:

> Take a pint of double cream, whip it well, and then add five or six ounces of pounded sugar; put it in your freezing-pot, work it well until it is smooth.[10]

Earlier traditional recipes included eggs, to give a smoother texture.

Through this simple but successful enterprise, other Italian food slowly entered the consciousness of the British public, and the increasing number

She. I think I should like ice-creams better if they were not so cold.

He. Should you my dear? Then I'd recommend you to have the chill taken off in future.

of humble 'cook's shops', as well as 'breakfast and tea houses for working men' and coffee shops also helped.[11] In time Italian produce became more widely available, and by 1868 some special items were listed as being available in Greek Street, Soho, at the shop of a famous importer of foreign food, B. Perelli-Rocco. There one could find 'the creamy butter of Milan imported every week', 'vast stores of macaroni, and lentils, and Italian cheeses and Bologna sausages, and tomato paste, all at very reasonable prices'. Another reputable Italian shop was that of Domenico Piccirillo of Broad Street (Oxford), who also traded out of Wigmore Street. In this part of London, the rising West End, a contemporary witness recalled the neighbourhood 'savoury with macaroni and oils, betokening the presence of the Italian element who flock to Soho Square in great numbers when they arrive in London'.[12]

Italian groceries were also springing up in Scotland. George Hill, of 45 North Frederick Street, Edinburgh was trading in 1844 as 'Italian warehouseman in Ordinary to the Queen', and by 1849 there were two branches of the Italian Grocery and Confectionery Warehouses in the Scottish capital, in Hanover Street and Rutland Place.[13] A John McKaig had opened an Italian warehouse in Dumfries by 1836 and two others are recorded in Glasgow and Kirkcudbright, a harbour town on the Solway coast.

THE UBIQUITOUS MACARONI

What now identified 'Italian food' in Britain was macaroni. Even if the top restaurants in London were dominated by French cuisine, and virtually all menus were written in French, many of the most important English recipe books of the mid nineteenth century started including a number of Italian dishes. Macaroni, spaghetti, vermicelli and ravioli appear more and more frequently on menus and in recipe books, with macaroni (frequently spelt *maccaroni*) invariably featuring most often, in soups or baked with cheese, as well as in other preparations. In America, an 1846 menu for the Astor House restaurant in New York even lists a complicated dish like timbale of macaroni.[14] Even the menus of quintessentially British institutions such as the thirty or so London gentlemen's clubs regularly included 'Italian pastes'.[15] W. B. Jerrold, the author of *The Epicure's Year Book and Table Companion* (1868), mentions among 'memorable menus' that at the Hotel Previtali, in Arundel Street, where he ate 'excellent macaroni and a few capital Italian dishes'; he found seasonal menus that included a 'Potage à l'Italienne' and 'Boudin à la Garibaldi' for July, 'Consommé aux lazanges' (August), 'Potage aux ravioli' (September) and for October some 'Potages aux pâtes d'Italie'.[16] Italian food also infiltrated many homes, although often, according to Jerrold, it did not go beyond 'a dismal attempt at maccaroni'.

MRS ACTON LEADS THE WAY

Eliza Acton, whom we have already met in Chapter 4, provided detailed instructions on the use of Naples and Genoa macaroni, but she also mentioned 'ribbon macaroni (*lazanges* [*sic*])' and even *macaroncini* 'not much larger than a straw' but requiring 'much boiling for its size'. She is one of the few to write about a 'celery-macaroni' which is 'made very large and of an ornamental form, but in short lengths. It is used by "professed" cooks as a sort of crust or case for *quenelle*-forcemeat, or other expensive preparations of the same nature.' Mrs Acton warns the home cook to avoid very white Italian pastes, which are of inferior quality, while the best have an unmistakable 'yellowish tint'. She recommends boiling the Naples macaroni for about three quarters of an hour, and the Genoa pasta for nearly an hour![17] The idea was that well-cooked pasta was easier to digest, although later it was discovered that the opposite is true. Certainly the concept of *al dente* pasta was still a long way off.

Mrs Acton's recipe for 'dressed macaroni' is particularly detailed. Since she is not very happy with the common use of just Parmesan cheese, butter and cream, she suggests finely flavoured English cheese instead, apparently to avoid lumps. While acknowledging the common English dressing of grated cheese, butter and cream, she also favours the use of very strong jelly gravy like the French, or tossing the macaroni in a rich brown gravy, like the Italians do, among 'their many other modes of serving it'.[18] It is interesting

de Cuisine, published nearly thirty years later, in 1873.

It is generally acknowledged that many recipes in Mrs Beeton's *Book of Household Management* owe a considerable amount to her predecessors, and particularly to Mr Soyer.[27] In the first edition of her famous book she also mentioned a few dishes, apart from macaroni, from various parts of Italy, such as 'Italian mutton cutlets', in which various savoury herbs are used as well as mace, a beaten yolk of egg, butter and breadcrumbs, a small quantity of tarragon vinegar and a little port. She also included some sweets, such as Savoy biscuits and cakes, and Italian cream. I wonder if Mrs Beeton deliberately ignored the dishes attributed to specific regions, such as Piedmont, Lombardy, the Venetian territory, Florence, Naples or Sicily because, after the unification of Italy in 1861, she thought there was no 'all-Italian' representative dish, apart from macaroni. Or maybe her knowledge of geography was rather vague.

In the United States a book of over 3,500 recipes by Charles Ranhofer, former chef of the celebrated Delmonico's restaurant in New York, included several Italian dishes, including gnocchi, macaroni 'Neapolitan style', spaghetti, ravioli 'à la Bellini' and risotto 'with Piedmontese truffles'.[28]

ITALIAN SWEET TREATS

Guglielmo (William) Alexis Jarrin was an Italian pastry chef born in 1784 in Colorno near Parma who worked in Paris and became one of the most accomplished confectioners of his times. He moved to England in 1817 and started running various confectionery establishments in London. When he published his book, *The Italian Confectioner* (1820), his shop was prestigiously sited at 123 Bond Street. Jarrin introduced various innovations in his art, such as the use of colours in ices, and the use of an ice-cream bombe mould – 'Neapolitan bombe' began to appear on elegant menus.[29] In the Preface he declared that he 'examined the principal works of the confectioner's art, published in Italy, Germany and France'. He also claimed that he tried to include in his treatise 'a variety of articles entirely new, and describing processes little, if at all, known in England'. His work encompasses sugar, candies, ices and ice-creams, jams and preserves, chocolate, liqueurs, 'Cakes, Wafers, Biscuits (particularly those of Italy), rich Cakes, Biscotini, Macaroons &c.'. To this mouthwatering list, one should add the numerous specific recipes for Italian biscuits he included (pistachio biscottini, mustacioli biscuits, Firenze biscuits and Savoy biscuits among others) and Italian cakes, including two slightly different recipes for a rich fruit cake typical of his native Emilia-Romagna, known as *spongata*, which he also presents as 'an Italian Christmas cake'.[30]

RECIPES FOR THE ITALIAN COMMUNITY

Some twenty years after Mrs Beeton's huge tome was published, a small collection of recipes specifically dedicated to the Italian community appeared in London. Nothing is known about the woman who published the book, Maria Gironci, who was probably a professional cook in London. Her English is at times quirky, and it is unclear whether she wrote the original recipes in English or, according to one surviving copy, she simply collected and translated them.[31] The first edition of her *Recipes of Italian Cookery* appeared in London in about 1883, and underwent various reprints, evidence of its success, mainly but not exclusively among the Italian community. The booklet was still in print in 1905.

The recipes were divided into five sections: Soups, Macaroni, Poultry and Game, Savoury Dishes and Sweet Dishes. In the titles of most recipes there was a certain attention to individual Italian regions. For example, among the soups we find 'Soup alla Romana', 'Soup alla Lombarda' and (to my delight) 'Soup alla Piacentina' – further on in the book two other recipes from Piacenza appear: 'Sauce alla Piacentina' and 'Duck alla Piacentina', although I have never heard of them before. Among the Italian Londoners there was a large number from the mountains south of Piacenza, and some of them may have contributed to this collection of essentially family dishes.[32]

The cooking time will depend on the age of the beans, but if after about 35 minutes they are tender, you can salt them and cook for another 5 minutes, before draining them, removing the celery and onion, and setting to one side.

Mix the flour and the fine breadcrumbs with some warm water and a good pinch of salt until you have a fairly stiff dough. Knead it for a while, at least ten minutes, until quite smooth. Roll a small piece of dough in your hands to make a short 'snake' roughly the diameter of your little finger. Cut the snake into small chunks, approximately 1cm (½in) in length, pressing each one fairly vigorously with your thumb, in an almost circular motion, on a wooden surface. You will obtain curly little dumplings, which you can set aside on a clean cloth or a surface sprinkled with flour, until the sauce is ready. If you wish, you can make these beforehand; they can be left for about six hours or even overnight, but should not be allowed to become too hard or dry.

You are now ready to prepare the sauce, ideally in a terracotta pot. Heat the remaining oil and the butter blended with a little chopped parsley and a little garlic. If I have no vegetarian guests, I like to use cured pork fat (*lardo*) for extra flavour. Lightly fry the chopped onion, then add garlic (if using), tomato paste diluted with a little hot water, salt and pepper, one or two sage leaves and a few basil leaves, and cook on a low heat for about ten minutes. Next, add the cooked borlotti beans with a little of the water in which they have cooked, together with the pork rind if you are including. Simmer for another ten minutes, or until the beans are completely tender. Check seasoning.

Bring plenty of salted water to the boil, then drop in the dumplings. As soon as they come bobbing to the surface, remove them with a slotted spoon and stir them into the sauce, either on individual plates or altogether in a large serving dish. You can add some grated Parmesan cheese on top, and I like the addition of some more freshly ground pepper.

It may sound complicated, but the result is delicious, and I recently tried this traditional dish in a good old *osteria* in Piacenza. You can hardly find the 'little willies' anywhere else! A glass of Barbera or a good Chianti would be a good choice to go with this dish, or in Piacenza one would have a mature Gutturnio.

In the introduction to her book, Maria Gironci stressed that

Attention has lately been drawn to Italian cookery, and in Mr Montague Williams valuable book on the 'Chemistry of Cooking',[33] mention is made of the want of Italian recipes, specially those with cheese, of which many will be found in this book. Maccaroni is now much more used in England by all classes, and complaints are made of the lack of recipes for cooking it; these will also be found in this book.

As an example of the numerous recipes dedicated to 'maccaroni', here's the one she provides according to the Neapolitan fashion:

MACCARONI ALLA NAPOLITANA

Cook in salted boiling water, 12 ounces of macaroni, well drain [*sic*], place on hot dish, pour over four ounces melted butter, mix in gradually six ounces grated cheese, the macaroni must be stirred with two forks, put it in layers on dish, and serve with grated cheese or sprinkle thickly over.[34]

Her recipe No. 123, entitled 'Maccaroni Stew alla Napolitana', looks like a cruder version of Eliza Acton's Neapolitan *stufato*.

It is interesting to note that, although in the section dedicated to sauces there are various recipes for tomato sauce, conserve of tomatoes etc., the recipes for macaroni do not seem to include tomatoes, except, perhaps, No. 120:

STEWED STEAK AND SPAGHETTI

Fry until brown in six ounces butter, one chopped onion, tablespoonful each of parsley and rosemary, add one pound and a half rump steak, cut into small square pieces, fry, turning the pieces for eight or ten minutes, then pour in the pan half tumbler red wine, pint of stock, with three ounces conserve of tomatoes dissolved in it, or the strained juice of six tomatoes, pepper and salt to taste, and teaspoonful mixed spice. Stew over slow fire for one hour or more. Have ready eight ounces cooked spaghetti, place meat in centre of dish, spaghetti round, pour sauce over. Serve with grated cheese.

Onion fried in butter produces a very distinctive smell, which to many northern Italians of my generation suggests that lunch is being prepared. Onions fried gently with a variety of other vegetables and herbs create *soffritto*, the foundation of so many Mediterrranean dishes, and expensive olive oil was not always used, unless it was for lightly frying garlic, which produces its own distinctive aroma, loved by some, disliked by many.

The recipes collected by Maria Gironci are simpler than those of most professional cooks; they seem transcribed from oral instructions and many dishes are an early example of 'Anglo-Italian fusion'. However, they contribute to helping our imagination reconstruct the smells that must have been common in the streets of London's Little Italy, the quarter situated to the north and south of where Clerkenwell Road lies today. It included the streets around Saffron Hill, Leather Lane and Hatton Garden. In 1890 Luigi Terroni, an Italian from the Tuscan town of Pontremoli, opened a food shop in Clerkenwell Road, close to the Italian church of St Peter's, and the Terroni family continued trading in the same location until 2007.

ITALIAN HOTELS AND RESTAURANTS IN LONDON

In a book published in 1899, Lieutenant-Colonel Newnham-Davis, one of the earliest food writers and gourmets in Britain, listed approximately 120 restaurants in London, of which seventeen were 'Italian' and a few more run by Italians, against twenty-three serving French food, three German and one Jewish. Four restaurants are also specified as 'vegetarian'.[35]

His book opens with an account of Romano's in the Strand, which was in fact a temple of French *haute cuisine*. However, even Romano had *spongada à la palermitaine* (a kind of Christmas cake) included in a specimen menu of a 'dinner of ceremony'. When the colonel moved on to Pagani's in Great Portland Street, one of the best known Italian restaurants in London, he found that the fish on the menu were accompanied by two Italian names – *filet de sole Pagani* and *turbot à la Pellegrini* – and he introduces some protagonists of Italian catering, Mr Giuseppe Pagani himself, and Mr Meschini his business partner (who wrote the recipe for the sole fillet), as well as Mr Notari, the chef, 'an artist in his kitchen'.

The sole recipe is worth quoting here, to appreciate the difference between the relative simplicity of twenty-first century treatment of fish, and the elaborate use of sauces in the belle époque:

> The sole is first of all filleted, and with the bones, some mussels, and a little white wine, a *fumée de poisson* [fish stock] is made in which the fillets of the sole are then cooked. The cook takes this *cuisson* [cooked preparation], and by adding some well-chopped fresh mushrooms, makes with that what he calls a *réduction*; to this he adds some *velouté* [a smooth, light stock sauce], a little cream, fresh butter, some lemon juice, pepper and salt, and cooks the whole together till well mixed, then passes it *à l'étamine* [through a strainer]. With this the sauce is made. The cooked fillets of sole and eight or ten mussels are then placed ready on a silver dish, and the above made sauce poured over them. The top is well sprinkled with fresh Parmesan cheese, and after allowing them to *gratiner* [grill] for a minute or two, are ready to be put on the customer's table.

After the sole, the colonel and his guest try some *tournedos truffés* (beef fillets with truffles), otherwise known as *tournedos à la Rossini*, deemed to be 'perfectly heavenly', and then a partridge and its casserole 'with all its savoury surroundings'. We can indeed follow the scent. They are obviously satisfied by the level of excellence achieved by all the dishes, although the colonel has a slight criticism of the soufflés. They effortlessly manage to drink two pints of

addition of a little salt, but no water. In some regions an egg is added to the flour, and the small dumplings are usually rolled out by pressing with your thumb on a fork, or on the back of a cheese grater, to make them lighter, exactly as indicated by a papal chef back in 1570, when of course potatoes were unknown. The gnocchi are then cooked in boiling water, although Nicolas Soyer recommends baking them with a little butter and Parmesan.

Rice is also quite popular in Nicolas's book, and many of his dishes are inspired by Italy, including 'rice *à l'italienne*' (boiled rice with butter) and rice fritters, which can be made with leftovers. There is a proper *risotto à la milanaise*, which does not include any wine or saffron, a risotto with tomatoes, and another risotto made with stock. A recipe for stewed rice and cabbage is reminiscent of a dish described by Dickens when travelling in northern Italy in 1846.[39]

With the arrival of the twentieth century, the scene is therefore set for an expansion of Italian food in England. There will be setbacks, especially because of the two World Wars, but small restaurants and homely trattorias will eventually be transformed into places where Hollywood stars, royalty and other celebrities, and not just them … will enjoy proper Italian food.

6. PIZZERIAS AND TRATTORIAS

PIZZA IS AN ANCIENT WORD, recorded for the first time in 997 BCE in the area of Naples, at Gaeta, and came to be used variously to describe 'a piece of bread', 'a thin-baked *focaccia*', 'a pointed piece of baked dough' or basically a flatbread. It is frequently connected with ancient Greek *pitta* or *pissa*, but the connection between these words meaning 'pitch', the bituminous substance, and a flatbread is far from convincing (though Alan Davidson in his *Oxford Dictionary of Food* maintains that pine resin, from which pitch was formed, is layered like flatbread). A legendary account of *pizza* has it being brought by Greeks and Albanians to southern Italy, and specifically to Calabria,[1] but a serious study of the origin of the word held that *pizza* appeared first in areas of Italy influenced by Longobard settlements, providing a likely connection with Old Germanic *bizan* ('bite') and modern German *Bisschen* ('a morsel, a mouthful'). So *pizza* may have more to do with the Old English *bita* from which 'bit' has derived, than with ancient Greek.[2] However, two scholars have tried to prove more recently that *pizza* is directly connected with a series of words belonging to a variety of Semitic languages, such as *pite, pita, pitta*, and they establish connections with ancient Aramaic and Syrian, in which those terms refer to 'bread'.[3]

For a long time, from the sixteenth century onwards, pizza also referred to a sweet cake, or maybe a pie, certainly without any tomatoes or cheese. Even in the nineteenth century, in the most famous and important cookery book published in Italy, commonly known as *L'Artusi*, the recipes for two pizzas, *pizza alla napoletana* and *pizza gravida* ('pregnant' pizza) refer to a mixture of short pastry with sugar, almonds, eggs and milk. A third, *pizza a libretti* (literally 'booklet pizza', but more usually called accordion cake), is a fried pastry with sugar on top.[4]

Whatever the ancient antecedents, there is no doubt that pizza as we know it originated in Naples. At first it was a 'white pizza', with a topping of fine lard and herbs (oregano, basil), or oil and cheese. The first known takeaway shops are recorded in 1727 and 1732 in Naples, and by around 1760 pizza was being improved with the addition of some fresh tomatoes and cheese. The first cheese to be used was probably *caciocavallo*, but was soon substituted with mozzarella. It was around this time that some pizzerias in Naples started to provide tables so that customers could sit down and eat.[5]

Pizza was considered a rustic dish sold by street vendors and eaten as a meal in the street, mainly by the poor. Alexandre Dumas, author of *The Three Musketeers*, who travelled to Naples in 1835, claimed that the *lazzaroni* (the poorest idlers) subsisted on two foods, according to the season: watermelon in summer and pizza in winter. He remarks that pizzas, which he found similar to a 'pastry (*talmouse*) made in Saint Denis, in a round shape and produced with bread dough', can be made 'with oil, with backfat, lard, cheese, tomatoes and small fish. [The pizza] is the gastronomic thermometer of the market: it goes up and down in price according to the cost of the ingredients just mentioned.' Naturally, a stale pizza was cheaper. Dumas also reported that for those who had very little money there was even week-old pizza for sale, which 'could be a substitute for a sailor's biscuit' – not very palatable but certainly cheap.[6]

While pizza became popular with all strata of society throughout the south of Italy – the King of Naples, Ferdinand II of Bourbon (1810–59) even had a pizza oven installed in the royal palace of Capodimonte – it did not reach other parts of Italy until much later, and some foreign travellers did not appreciate it at all. Samuel Morse, the inventor of the telegraph code, tried a pizza in 1831 and described it as a loathsome local speciality:

a species of most nauseating looking cake … covered over with slices of *pomodoro* or tomatoes, and sprinkled with little fish and black pepper and I know not what other ingredients, it altogether looks like a piece of bread that had been taken reeking out of the sewer.[7]

Some Italian visitors from further north were not impressed either. The author of *Pinocchio*, Carlo Collodi, who came from Florence, lingered in his description on the 'blackened aspect of its toasted crust, the whitish sheen of garlic and anchovy, the greenish-yellow tint of the oil and fried herbs, and the bits of red from the tomato here and there'. He added that this altogether gave the pizza 'the appearance of complicated filth that matches the dirt of the vendor'.[8]

Caciocavallo: the original cheese used for pizza

However, it appears that a turning point came in the summer of 1889, when the King and Queen of Italy, Umberto and Margherita of Savoy, visited Naples and decided to try the local speciality. One of the top pizza cooks in town, Raffaele Esposito, was summoned to prepare a variety of pizzas for the Queen, and he offered three: with lard, *caciocavallo* and basil; with oil and tiny fish, a kind of newly born sardine known locally as *cecenielle*; and with tomatoes, mozzarella, oil and basil. The Queen chose the last one, because – the story goes – the colours were those of the Italian flag, red, white and green. At the time, this was known as *pizza alla mozzarella*, but from then on it became known as *pizza Margherita* after the Queen. In the Pizzeria Da Pietro (now Pizzeria Brandi), where Raffaele worked, one can still admire the thank-you letter signed by the Head of the Table of the Royal Household dated June 1889.

A few years later another celebrity from northern Italy, Guglielmo Marconi, who had just patented his wireless telegraph, visited Naples before leaving for America, and decided to try a pizza, which was still largely unknown outside the south. He chose the best place in town (Pizzeria Brandi, as it happens) and when he finished his meal, he was asked by the waiter about his impression. The great inventor replied that he had enjoyed his pizza but had had some trouble with the stringy cheese. At that point the quick-witted waiter retorted: 'Your Excellency should have invented the wireless mozzarella, instead of the wireless telegraph!'

TRANSATLANTIC TRANSLATIONS

Pizza was introduced to the United States by Italian immigrants at the end of the nineteenth century. The first official pizzeria licensed by the authorities was opened in 1905 in New York by Gennaro Lombardi. This catered mainly to Italian-Americans, but the pizza's success was relatively quick, due to the low cost of its ingredients and the demand in immigrant areas. By the 1930s most of the Italian neighbourhoods in eastern coastal cities had taverns and shops selling pizzas.[9] In 1943 Ric Ricardo of Pizzeria Uno in Chicago invented the deep-dish pizza – bigger is better? – baked in a deep metal pan, with thick dough and a lavish use of disparate ingredients. The success of pizza was also helped along by soldiers returning from southern Italy after the war in 1945. Some would also have had mechanical and engineering aptitudes, and one went on to patent a new gas-fired pizza oven. Before then, most ovens were fired with wood or coal.

By the 1950s, pizza was an all-American food. The lyrics of 'That's Amore', sung by the actor Dean Martin (who was of Italian parentage, born Dino Paul Crocetti), sounded like an advertisement for the Italian–American dish: 'When the moon hits your eye like a big pizza pie, that's amore!' Dean crooned – apparently reluctantly, since he believed that it was a 'very silly song', despite its popularity.[10] The same song mentions another Italian dish that was also part of the Italian–American menu: 'When the stars make you drool just like pasta fazool, That's amore.'[11] But pasta with beans is a dish which, although found with infinite variations all over Italy and part of the stereotyped image of the Italian immigrant, never hit the spotlight like pizza.

As an aside, there was one national, and eventually international, boom in a range of Italian food that wasn't pizza. A very young cook from Piacenza, Ettore Boiardi, emigrated to the States in 1914 to join his brother in the catering business. He worked in top hotels in New York, became head chef of the Plaza Hotel and also once prepared a dinner for President Wilson. In 1924 he opened his own restaurant, Il Giardino d'Italia in Cleveland, where some customers asked for portions 'to take away'. Boiardi started selling a kind of pasta kit to be used in domestic kitchens, then decided to prepare spaghetti with tomato sauce and Parmesan cheese in tins. With the help of sponsors, he started selling his pasta products commercially under the name of Chef BOY-AR-DEE, and achieved fantastic success in the late 1920s. During the Second World War, he provided tinned pasta to American troops, and other provisions to the Russian Army. After the war he widened his range of Italian products, and Boiardi's pre-cooked spaghetti and ravioli reached the UK in the 1960s.[12] They may not have been readily recognizable as proper Italian food, but they did introduce a large number of people to pasta with tomato or meat sauce, and probably revived the word *ravioli*, mentioned for the first time in 1598 by John Florio (see Chapter 2). An Anglo–Italian friend of old times recently confirmed that Boiardi's ravioli was actually quite good.

The spread of pizza in America was given an extra boost in 1957 when the Celentano brothers started marketing frozen pizza that you could cook at home. The following year two other brothers, Frank and Dan Carney, opened the first Pizza Hut; a decade later there were 310 stores across the United States, and in the 1980s the brand went global. It was yet another pair of brothers, Tom and James Monaghan (what is it with brothers and pizza?), who started Domino's, originally known as Dominick's, in Ypsilanti, Michigan. They were the first to start delivering pizzas to customers' homes, first in university towns and then all over the United States.[13] By 1970 what had started as a marginal ethnic food had become the favourite snack food of Americans in their twenties, and coming straight after hamburgers and cheeseburgers for the rest of the population.[14] As well as a presence on every Main Street, pizzas and pizzerias entered popular culture and had roles in films from *Saturday Night Fever* (1977) to *Mystic Pizza* (1988). American pizza fans maintain that Italians may have brought pizza to the States, but America introduced it to the world.

VERACE PIZZA NAPOLETANA

The great international success of pizza prompted a group of Neapolitans to found the Association for True Neapolitan Pizza in June 1984. In 1997 its members successfully campaigned to have this traditional dish given an official Certification of Origin as 'the true Neapolitan pizza (DOC)'. *Denominazione di origine controllata* (DOC) is similar to the *Appellation Contrôlée* for French wines and other products and is a quality assurance label that means a product has been made according to strict regulations. In 2010, the product 'Pizza Napoletana' received the trademark of 'Traditional Guaranteed Speciality', and in 2016 Italy put Neapolitan pizza forward for UNESCO recognition as 'Intangible Cultural Heritage of Humanity'. This was confirmed in December 2017.

Professor Carlo Mangoni of Naples University, one of the founders of the Association, was awarded a substantial grant to draw up the technical specifications for *Verace Pizza Napoletana* (true Neapolitan pizza), VPN for short. This runs to over eleven pages, and specifies the type of flour which should be used (00 flour, with a very small amount of Manitoba type 0 flour), the type of water (with limited calcium), the type of yeast (brewer's), the type of tomatoes to be used (St Marzano, or other tomatoes from Campania, but peeled tinned tomatoes are allowed). There are only two types of pizza which can be called Neapolitan: *marinara*, with tomato, extra virgin olive oil, garlic and oregano; and *Margherita*, with tomato, extra virgin olive oil, mozzarella (from buffalo milk, or cow's milk known as *fior di latte*), a few grams of grated hard cheese and a few leaves of basil. These are usually baked in a scorching oven – the temperature required is 430°C (800°F) – for about

60–90 seconds. Pizzerias around the world can apply for the certification from the Association, and can then display a special VPN badge if they have met all the specifications.[15]

Such a pizza cannot really be made at home, because normal domestic ovens do not reach the required temperature, but I have recently learnt of a small portable but powerful electric oven on the market that can do the trick, and friends from Bologna have assured me it works very well. It can only cook one pizza at a time, but each one only takes three minutes.

PREVENTION OF CRUELTY TO FOOD

When I first visited London in the early Sixties, I do not remember being aware of pizzerias. There were spaghetti houses, and a few other 'Italian' trattorias, but my student budget did not allow me to be very adventurous. By the end of the decade, when I used to go regularly to the British Museum Library, I remember eating fairly frequently at a Pizza Express on the corner of Great Russell Street. The first Pizza Express (still in existence in Soho's Wardour Street) was opened in 1965 by entrepreneur Peter Boizot, who relied on the Italian artist and designer Enzo Apicella for a new look. In just a few years more than 300 Pizza Express restaurants had opened in the UK. They had a variety of pizzas on the menu, apart from the traditional Neapolitan, and chefs assembled the pizzas from fresh ingredients, so the experience was rather better than eating at a fast food joint. Decent Italian wines were on offer and the whole setting was somewhat chic.

Pizza had been available in London since the early 1950s, but its consumption was largely confined to Italian immigrants, and there is no mention of pizzerias in the earliest edition of *The Good Food Guide* (1951–2), although a *pizza napoletana* could be found in Hampstead Continental Restaurant. Similarly, *Bon Viveur's London* (1954) mentions *pizza alla romana* offered by Ciccio in Kensington along with *gnocchi romaine*, usually made with semolina, as well as somewhat expensive *saltimbocca alla zingara* (slivers of veal with cheese and wine) and real zabaglione.[16]

e best spaghetti bolognese in Soho'. This last is something that Italians still
use to accept as a proper Italian dish, since real, slowly cooked bolognese
at sauce should only be paired with tagliatelle. The restaurant that offered
largest number of Italian dishes was another Soho establishment: Quo
is, the creation of 'Papà Leoni'. Here you could sample 'Pollo alla Yolanda
cken with cheese and asparagus tips]' and 'Calves Head Florio' [no
anation is provided for this dish] and 'Lasagne verdi' (green lasagne),
ll as 'Minestrone, Pollo Romana, Ravioli, Tagliatelli and Risotto'. At
me of writing Quo Vadis is still a successful restaurant and a private
ers' club in Dean Street, with an eclectic and varied menu.
in all, in 1950s Britain reconstruction was under way, the economy was
improving, and many people, after years of austerity, longed to try new
including foreign foods and wine.

Pizz

In the 1950s, food rations imposed in the UK during the Second World
War came to an end, with the last restrictions on bacon and meat lifted on
3 July 1954, later than in any other European country.[17] In 1948 an eminent
Italian poet, Eugenio Montale, visited England twice together with the
novelist Alberto Moravia. In lively journalistic prose, Montale expressed the
difficulties of eating in Britain, where everything was rather meagre. Among
other things, he mentions an Irish stew, which he said appeared to be made
with old goat's meat, rather chewy and interspersed with a few overcooked
and tasteless vegetables.[18]

In hotels and restaurants, according to some who worked in the catering
trade, 'the Second World War had become the perfect excuse for a lack of
everything, including courtesy' and on the whole standards were very low.[19]
There was, however, a beacon of Italian taste in the form of a burgeoning
coffee culture. In 1949 Lou and Caterina Polledri opened Bar Italia in Frith
Street, Soho. Lou, who was originally from Piacenza, had already opened
a small café, but this new bar, with its shiny new Gaggia espresso machine,
became a meeting place for everybody interested in Italian drink and food,

kitchen facilities, she agreed to freeze her own prepared food, such as some delicious lasagne or a flavoursome chicken stock made with fresh onions, carrots and herbs from her own vegetable garden and a mature hen bought from some neighbours in the country.

Yet, even in the late 1950s, several years after Elizabeth David opened the eyes of the British to the delights of southern European cuisine, direct knowledge of Italian staples was still limited to a middle-class minority. On 1 April 1957, it was still possible for Richard Dimbleby, the BBC presenter who had covered the coronation of Queen Elizabeth four years earlier, to announce in a short BBC 'Panorama' report that the spaghetti farmers in Italy were anxious for their crops, because of frost at the end of March. The film showed long strands of spaghetti being cut from luscious trees and carefully put into baskets to dry by 'Italian peasant girls' in traditional costumes. Many people fell for this April Fool's hoax, given the authority of the presenter, and the BBC received call after call enquiring how to grow spaghetti. In the end the BBC switchboard operators came up with a standard response to enquiries, and suggested callers plant 'a sprig of spaghetti in a tin of tomato and hope for the best'.[20]

Things were changing, but it was still far from easy to experiment with foreign food. As Elizabeth David, writing just after the end of food rationing, put it:

Maybe you could at last buy veal, but if your butcher knew how to cut escalopes you were lucky. The purchase of a supply of olive oil, and for that matter even a small amount of Parmesan in the piece, entailed a bus trip to the Italian provision shops of Soho and heavily laden shopping bags to tote home. Still, the efforts involved did make cooking and entertaining in those days very rewarding and enjoyable.[21]

Pasta shapes from a folded leaflet advertising 117 different types of D'Apuzzo pasta. *Premiato Pastificio 'San Vincenzo', c.1950*

160

At least two of those Italian provision shops should be mentioned as historical monuments to Italian food in London's Soho. Lina Stores was established in 1940 by a lady from Genoa but was soon passed on to Giovanni and Rosa Filippi, a couple from Vernasca, in the hills south of Piacenza. I remember occasionally talking to the owners in my own dialect, while choosing dried broad beans from a jute sack – yes, it is still within living memory that old grocery shops would be full of jute sacks of pulses, rice, salt fish and other dried goods. In 2010, as I was strolling along Brewer Street, just outside Lina's shop, I was given a card which announced that after seventy years of trading, Lina Stores had decided to 'try "this internet" and start selling online'. Recently the shop has been completely modernized and, it seems to me, turned into a smaller place with fewer items over the counter, presumably because sales online have increased.

The other historic Italian delicatessen I must mention is Camisa, which opened in Soho's Berwick Street in 1929 (since 1960 they have been established just round the corner in Old Compton Street). The original Camisa & Sons came from the Apennines in the district of Parma. I used to pay regular visits to their rather cramped shop before a wide range of Italian products became available in mainstream supermarkets or online. Their supply of salami, Parma ham, mortadella, Gorgonzola, and a wide variety of pasta, rice and dried beans has delighted many people who wanted to sample the real thing. I visited Camisa very recently and the shop arrangement has remained exactly the same as in the 1970s, with many of the items you would find in a good grocery shop in Italy.

NEW IDEAS, NEW TRATTORIAS

Apart from an increasing availability of authentic ingredients from Italy, many still of variable quality, changes were also taking place in the catering world.

Pasta shapes from a folded leaflet advertising 117 different types of D'Apuzzo pasta. *Premiato Pastificio 'San Vincenzo', c.1950*

The majority of Italian immigrants who reached Britain after the Second World War looked for jobs as waiters. The number of restaurants was increasing and the mantra was still that of 'French chefs in the kitchen, Italian staff in the restaurant'.[22] Many waiters, especially the ones who had been trained in top hotels, dreamed of opening their own restaurant one day, and quite a few managed to do so.

It was a difficult life, especially for newcomers. The first priority for any waiter who had just arrived was to learn the language, and it wasn't easy. An anecdote illustrates this problem graphically. The story goes that one day a young waiter, who was still on trial, was asked to do the breakfast shift. His English was non-existent but he would listen carefully to the customers' orders and then repeat the words to himself phonetically, without really understanding the meaning, until he could reach the chef. So, when a customer ordered 'egg, bacon, mushrooms, tomatoes and a sausage', the waiter memorized everything and spilled out to the cook: 'egg, bacon, mushrooms, tomatoes and a sausage'. The cook listened and then simply replied: 'no fockin' sausage'. The poor waiter obligingly returned to the customer and, quite innocently, reported the cook's exact words. The customer's reaction has not been passed down to us – let's hope he had a sense of humour. Sadly, there is also evidence that some waiters were treated rather badly at times.[23]

In the 1950s Italian restaurants had still been rather basic, mostly family-run affairs, with a few traditional Italian dishes on offer. But with the arrival of the new decade, the ten-year-old *Good Food Guide* was recommending twenty-two Italian restaurants in London, from Bertorelli's in Charlotte

Surf Naples, cartoon by Enzo Apicella

Street to Zia Teresa in Kensington, whose tagliatelle, gnocchi and lasagne were all commended, as was her pizza and the veal escalopes in the Neapolitan or Milanese fashion. One newish trattoria, Dei Pescatori, specialized in fish, and the 'Lasagne Don Camillo' was considered their best pasta dish. (Check out the Don Camillo books if you're curious about how this fish and cream dish got its name.) Other places were offering southern dishes such as *saltimbocca* (rolls of veal, ham and cheese) and *entrecôte alla pizzaiola* (steak with tomatoes, garlic and oregano).

But one southern Italian restaurant stood out above all others in the *Guide*, which reported in its 1961 edition:

> The restaurant is always crowded and the air of bustle and good humour adds to the enjoyment of your meal ... members praise baby octopus in sauce, grilled scampi on a skewer, stuffed chicken breast.[24]

Egon Ronay, in his guide the same year, also praised this 'tiny restaurant' where 'sports shirts take the place of stain-covered tails, silk lampshades give way to indirect lighting'. The ambience was lively and modern, the decor had a new look, and the food was exciting. This was a trattoria for up-and-coming 'swinging London'.

Who was behind this much lauded new eatery? It was created by two Italian waiters, Mario Cassandro from Naples and Franco Lagattolla from a Neapolitan family but born in England. They both had experience in high-class establishments such as the Savoy and the Mirabelle, and when they met by chance they decided to set up something new in London.

They pooled their savings, managed to obtain a substantial bank loan and, conscious of the risks they were taking, threw themselves into their new venture with real gusto. On 2 June 1959 a sign on the pavement outside 19 Romilly Street in Soho read:

> Mario & Franco's Trattoria Terrazza.
> Genuine Italian cooking.
> Moderate prices, opening tonight 6.00 o'clock.

The informality and bonhomie of Mario, as well as his ability to understand the financial difficulties that some young people might be experiencing, helped persuade a large number of customers to open monthly accounts with the restaurant. This was an innovative system before the arrival of credit cards. The 'Trat', as it became known among its fans, attracted the attention of numerous celebrities of the time, who were brought in by some of Mario and Franco's early regulars, including the restaurant's designer, Enzo Apicella, and by people working in the film studios nearby. Many young artists, writers, film stars, politicians and aristocrats ate there, including Frank Sinatra, who came in with a large party of friends. Many years later, the *Guardian* summed up the achievement of Mario's work in his obituary:

> Mario Cassandro changed the face, as well as the taste and social attitudes, of London restaurants. With his partner, Franco Lagattolla, he created a brand of raffish Neapolitan elegance that caught the 1960s zeitgeist perfectly. When *Time* magazine published its famous 1966 issue about swinging London, and reported that 'a new eating style is visible on all sides', it was to Mario and Franco's trattoria La Terrazza in Soho – 'the Trat', as it was known – that the world flocked to dine, lunch and rubberneck.[25]

Their 'secret' was simple and was revealed by Franco in his book of recipes: 'Use only the finest ingredients, and the freshest of everything. The best results depend on those two factors perhaps more than any other.'[26]

One of their most popular dishes, a kind of signature dish, was *petto di pollo sorpresa* (chicken breast surprise), priced at 9s 6d in 1961. It was defined by Egon Ronay as 'an Italianised and slightly garlicky version of chicken Kiev', an adaptation invented by Franco. The surprise of the dish was the possibility that the hot butter might spurt out – the waiters always asked customers if they wanted it cut, since many who refused went home with well-buttered ties. Here is the recipe, reproduced from Franco's book:

166

PETTO DI POLLO SORPRESA

Serves 4

First, ask your butcher to cut and skin four tender breasts of young chicken, preferably free range, leaving the wing-tip bone. Carefully, without breaking the flesh, flatten them with a flat-sided mallet-cleaver, very, very thinly.

Place a 50g conical-shaped piece of well-chilled butter, which has been mixed with finely chopped garlic and parsley, a teaspoonful of grated Parmesan cheese, salt and milled black pepper, in the centre of each piece of chicken.

In December 1962 Mario and Franco decided to challenge the top French restaurants in London with a high class, utterly contemporary restaurant, designed yet again in a minimalist style by Enzo Apicella. Tiberio in Mayfair's Queen Street was a luxury establishment that was soon recognized by critics as being on a par with the capital's top French restaurants, Mirabelle, Le Coq d'Or or Le Caprice, and in a food column published in *Queen* magazine in 1966, the journalist Quentin Crewe wrote: 'I can't think of a restaurant in London which gives one more strongly the sensation that they want you to enjoy yourself – they want you to like the food and want you to feel that dinner here is an occasion.'[28]

The example of Mario and Franco was to be followed by scores of members of their staff, who in due course opened their own Italian trattorias in London.[29] And the enhanced reputation of Italian food and restaurants spread even to the outer reaches of Britain. Valvona & Crolla, opened by

7. FROM MARKETS TO SUPERMARKETS

ONCE UPON A TIME, to the average Brit a sandwich was two slices of chalky white bread with some rubbery cheese and limp lettuce in between. Nowadays we are more likely to be found tucking into a ciabatta roll crammed with prosciutto and radicchio or a grilled panini oozing mozzarella.[1] The options available to us have increased exponentially, and this explosion of choice has only really happened in the last fifty years. How did this come about?

The 1970s introduced the era of cheap charter flights, and with more people holidaying abroad, the British were becoming more familiar with foreign cuisines. Joining the European Economic Community in 1973, and the relaxation of customs control it brought, made the exchange of goods much easier than before, even if it took much longer for some 'prohibited meats' such as salami and other cured pork or beef products to be allowed into the country.[2] Some people, including well-known chefs, admit that a little culinary smuggling may have taken place.[3] I was once called in by Dover Post Office because some 'condemned meat' addressed to me had been found in a parcel from Italy – I was asked to re-package the offending *coppa* and send it back to my mother.

The first item of Italian food to reach a large number of people was probably pasta, in the form of tinned spaghetti and ravioli, but quite early on good quality, durum wheat spaghetti, bucatini, linguine and tagliatelle started to appear in supermarkets. And soon many more goodies were to arrive.[4]

Although it was still difficult to find specific, sometimes basic items, Italian recipe books helped to spread the word, and stimulate the demand for new ingredients and intriguing ways of cooking them.

OFF TO A GOOD START: FRESH FOOD, SLOW FOOD

After Elizabeth David's books, another influential but almost forgotten collection of recipes was published by Patience Gray in 1957. *Plats du jour* sold over 150,000 copies in three years.[5] Despite its title (French was still the language of menus), it contained detailed information on Italian dishes. The care with which Gray provides information on ravioli and on the reasons why it is worth taking the trouble to make the little parcels at home, along with the methods for making the stuffing and the 'paste', are commendable.[6]

The fortunes of Italian cuisine received a further boost thanks to Marcella Hazan, an Italian who had emigrated to America and later opened a cookery school in Venice. In 1973 her book, *The Classic Italian Cook Book*, came out in the USA and was widely acclaimed. The book is divided thematically, as if it were following an elaborate dinner, starting with sauces, followed by antipasti, and then first and second courses, vegetables, salads, the cheese course, desserts and fruit, and finally 'afterthoughts' in which she suggests that 'what people do with food is an act that reveals how they construe the world ... The essential quality of Italian food can be defined as fidelity to its ingredients, to their taste, colour, shape and freshness.' She then adds a mild warning and a high-spirited remark: 'Because Italian cooking simply does not work without raw materials of the freshest and choicest quality, it is sometimes the most costly of the world's cuisines to produce. But it is probably the one whose satisfactions are the most accessible to the home cook.'[7] Marcella Hazan is generally credited with starting the craze for balsamic vinegar, something that, apparently, she later regretted. It is an ingredient that can now be found in all supermarkets, and that is likely to be provided, together with olive oil, in the better class of self-catering accommodation.

Balsamic vinegar in barrels, Modena

Most common balsamic vinegar is little more than a sweet, dark type of wine vinegar made with added caramel, but the real deal, *Aceto balsamico tradizionale di Modena*, is a very expensive syrupy condiment produced only in the Modena and Reggio Emilia area. It is made with cooked grape juice from a few specific grape varieties from Emilia-Romagna and left to mature for years in small wooden barrels. Some producers even have preferences in their choice of barrel wood. At the 2018 Salone del Gusto (Slow Food) in Turin I was able to compare real balsamics and there were indeed very subtle differences between one matured in, say, beech and another in (unusually) mulberry wood![8]

In 1980 Marcella Hazan's book was adapted for a British readership by Anna Del Conte. Anna Del Conte is one of the most revered and influential people among food writers. She is recognized by top British chefs as their inspiration for putting decent, traditional, simple Italian food on their menus. In 1976 she published *Portrait of Pasta*, in which she explained that in Italy there was much more than just spaghetti and tomato sauce.[9] Her clear, straightforward and persuasive recipes introduced several dishes that could be prepared at home. A decade later Anna published her fundamental *Gastronomy of Italy*, which received high praise and an international prize named after the Duchess of Parma. It is an unusual book, part recipe book and part encyclopedia of Italian foods, ingredients, kitchen utensils, local names of individual dishes and information on influential gastronomes. The entries are arranged in alphabetical order and they cover dishes and objects from every Italian region. In her introduction Anna Del Conte says that she hopes her passion for Italian food would succeed in persuading many non-Italians 'to love Italian food for all the fascination it offers, as well as for the eating of it'.

The *Gastronomy of Italy* had two further editions, in 2001 and 2013, after the original in 1987. Altogether Anna Del Conte published twelve books, including some biographical volumes. She always refused to participate in TV programmes, preferring to teach by example and by writing. At the age of 91, in a BBC2 celebratory programme, she explained that, when she moved to Britain in 1949, she found 'a culinary wasteland' and started thinking of remedying it.[10] First and foremost she felt that at the heart of Italian food was shopping, trying to find good-quality ingredients, but at the time there was 'no mozzarella, no ricotta, no mascarpone'. By the time her *Gastronomy* came out, the situation had considerably improved, and even supermarkets were providing good, genuine ingredients.

Across the Atlantic 'the greatest food writer who has ever lived, or at least written in English', as Simon Schama called her,[11] had outlined the principles of a personal, sensual and new approach to food back in the 1940s. For a long time Mary Frances Kennedy (M. F. K.) Fisher's voice was that of a lone wolf (one of her many books was entitled *How to Cook a Wolf!*), but by the 1970s things were changing in the USA too. Alice Waters was a pioneer advocate of the freshest vegetables, free-range eggs, seasonality and of sourcing high quality, preferably organic and local produce. Her culinary philosophy was influenced early on by the Montessori educational method, according to which you learn more by doing than by reading about it.[12] When she founded her restaurant, Chez Panisse in Berkeley, California, in 1971, a few years after the students' unrest, her ideas were regarded as suspiciously revolutionary. But she became very influential after opening the Chez Panisse Café in 1980.

Alice Waters' views are spelt out very clearly in her website: 'the best tasting food is organically and locally grown.' Vegetable growing should be respectful of the environment and only produce 'just out of the garden' should be presented to customers; fruit should be 'right off the branch', just as fish should arrive straight from the sea. To follow her principles, a close network of local, reliable, committed growers was created, none of them much further than an hour's drive from Berkeley. Alice Waters always felt that her views were shared by the Slow Food movement, and in 2002 she became the vice-president of Slow Food International.

This movement, which was started in Piedmont towards the end of the 1980s as a direct antagonist of fast food, was organized by a small group of friends led by Carlo Petrini. Over the years it has become more and more effective in advertising the importance of good food shared in a community, while encouraging consumers to be more aware of the origin of what they buy and what is put on their plates. According to Petrini, the producers, especially young farmers and wine providers, should be respected and should have an adequate reward. That is why food, for him and his world movement, should be 'good, clean and fair', the current mantra of the Slow Food movement. And it is not an empty slogan, since the movement is helping to create school gardens all over the world, in which children can learn to cultivate some of their own food, and have fun as well.[13] Petrini and his associates maintain that organic produce can be grown in many varied localities with different types of soil and weather situations, and with respect for sustainable and renewable sources.[14]

THE BEST DIET: EAT ITALIAN!

Apart from the influence of individual chefs and campaigners, there were other factors at work in the 1970s that helped to promote Italian food. It was being studied as a typical example of a 'Mediterranean diet', and endorsed by GPs and scientists.

In 1974 a UK pressure group known as Technology Assessment Consumerism Centre (TACC) strongly attacked the nutritional value of the white loaf (which I have always intensely disliked), and pointed out its lack of fibre and micronutrients. *The Times* published an article on unhealthy food with the heading 'Should bread carry a Government Health warning?', and for many it must have been a revelation that white bread was converted to sugar soon after being digested. Official committees recommended increased fibre in our diets, and towards the end of the decade too much fat, sugar and salt were directly linked to heart disease, cancer, obesity and other horrible things. In 1983 a series of articles in *The Sunday Times* recommended the need to reduce fat, sugar, salt and alcohol and to increase the intake of vegetable protein. It looked as if the triumph of the 'Mediterranean diet' was nigh.[15] To live a long and a better life, it was suggested by authoritative sources, choose Italian food!

The film star Sophia Loren had been an early part of this message, when she published her recipe book which included traditional recipes, especially pasta, meat and vegetable dishes from her native Naples (*Eat with me*, the English translation, appeared in 1972). She also added some 'digressions' in which she spoke passionately in favour of 'genuine food', stressing the importance of the freshness of the ingredients while recognizing the value of food technology and of the 'many good things in tins and frozen foods'.[16] She encouraged home cooks to 'rediscover the pleasure of cooking', in a kitchen which should be the realm of imagination. Many of her instructions are practical, such as advising readers on how to cook a fried pizza, since you cannot have a proper pizza oven in the house. She gave detailed instructions (which she calls Commandments) on how to cook good quality pasta *al dente*, and stressed the importance of doing something special for your guests, adding that 'taste, the proper flavour of a meal, is more than a part of the dishes which compose it'.[17]

Numerous books since, along with magazines, newspaper supplements, radio and TV programmes and, later, social media and blogs have provided recipes and encouragement for home cooks. Publications in both Britain and America have contributed to making specific Italian regions the focus of good life and good food, and their success indicates how hungry (literally and metaphorically) people are to learn. Frances Mayes' *Under the Tuscan Sun* is just a single example. When her book about finding her dream home came out in 1996 it sold millions of copies and six years later was made into a film. She followed it with other evocative books about the region and in 2012 with *The Tuscan Sun Cookbook*.

A KITCHEN REVOLUTION

A substantial contribution to the success of Italian dishes in England came from The River Café. It was opened in 1987 by Rose Gray and Ruth Rogers, who had spent time in central Italy, studying and experimenting with local cuisine. Their restaurant was soon patronized by top politicians, artists and royalty. In the introduction to their book, the authors expressed the feeling of revelation when faced with ingredients discovered during long periods spent in Tuscany:

> We were overwhelmed by the enormous variety of produce available in Italian food shops – the local pecorinos, the different types of prosciuttos and salamis, the smoked and salted pancettas, olive oils made by local farms, and olives preserved in brine. There were inviting sacks of dried beans – borlotti, fave [broad beans], cannellini and ceci [chickpeas]. In the vegetable markets we found tiny fennel bulbs which could be eaten raw, huge dense bunches of cicoria [chicory], stalls that sold only herbs, garlic or wild leaves.[18]

This was written in 1995, and the authors state clearly that just eight years before, when they had decided to open the restaurant, 'obtaining the right

Antonio Carluccio outside his Covent Garden restaurant, c.2015

ingredients was a challenge'. That's why they decided to bring back from Italy seeds of *cavolo nero*, an essential ingredient of some Tuscan recipes such as *ribollita*, and persuaded an organic gardener to grow this black kale for their restaurant. In 1995 it was much easier to obtain good mozzarella directly from Italy, and excellent olive oils were now available in England, along with pasta and polenta flours, as well as first-class Italian wines.[19] Nowadays, *cavolo nero* is available on many vegetable stalls in local markets, both organic and non-organic, as well as in a number of supermarkets. Gardeners began to grow radicchio, fennel and zucchini, in addition to special varieties of Italian tomatoes, such as *pomodori di Pachino*, which normally grow in Sicily.[20]

Even specialized varieties of chicory, such as the speckled Castelfranco from north-eastern Italy, started to appear on menus.[21] Italian flat-leaf parsley has been grown in England since the 1980s, and sold along many other herbs which once came only from Italy, Spain and Israel. Even small artichokes can now be found on local farms, and rare varieties of mild garlic such as the giant elephant garlic, which in Tuscany is known as *aglione*, are now grown in Britain where the climate permits.

The discovery of new vegetables also brought a renewed interest in wild food: nettles, dandelions, wild garlic, wild mushrooms. Foraging, which had never lost its appeal in much of continental Europe, became trendy, and among the first to launch wild British fungi was chef, restaurateur and writer of cookery books Antonio Carluccio. His menus listed a number of dishes with varieties of mushrooms never seen before on British tables. In his book *A Passion for Mushrooms* (1991), he illustrated numerous recipes that called for morels, parasol mushrooms, bay boletus, ink caps, chanterelles, truffles and *Boletus edulis*, better known in Italian as *porcini*.

The prized *porcini* probably derive their name, which means 'piglets', from an old Latin label (*Suillus fungus*, meaning 'piggish toadstool'), maybe because these mushrooms were loved by swine. These plump fungi, known as *cèpes* in French and penny buns or simply ceps in English, can easily be found in many English woods, but most people would refer to them simply as 'toadstools'. They are very elusive, though, and need the right level of humidity and warmth, as well as the right combination of trees (beech and oaks, for example), to reproduce. They are beautiful, elegant and fragrant, and on the continent are frequently dried and sold in small packets, to use in sauces, soups and risottos. I started picking them in Italy when I was about six, following my father in the woods. To spot a nice *porcino* was always a surprise and gave a great sense of achievement. Once, and only once, I managed to find twelve beauties, all under one bush, in the mountains south of Piacenza, to the envy of the other mushroom gatherers. They are now widely available in British supermarkets and delicatessens.

Another influential writer is Claudia Roden, who included numerous regional recipes, from Piedmont to Calabria, Sicily and Sardinia in her *The*

Food of Italy, published in 1989. Each section is preceded by a thorough introduction outlining the main features of the region's gastronomy. Again, the emphasis is on good quality, fresh ingredients and care in the preparation of individual dishes.

In the next decade, a young sous-chef who had worked with Carluccio and with the founders of The River Café, became a keen advocate of Italian food. Jamie Oliver was spotted by a BBC crew and started his TV career in 1999, aged 24, as 'The Naked Chef'.[22] The programme ran for three series and the book, with the same title, became a number one bestseller in the UK. That was the first of over twenty books written by Jamie Oliver, who enthuses about pasta and other things Italian, and always recognizes the teaching of his mentor Gennaro Cataldo, who also appeared on TV with Carluccio in 'Two Greedy Italians'.

In the introduction to his first book Oliver mentions the constraints of working in a very small kitchen while trying to re-create some exciting restaurant recipes. He started stripping down those recipes to something quite basic, and adapting them to what was available. One of the secrets of his success was the lack of culinary jargon, and flexibility in creating 'simple, delicious and feisty recipes'. He also talked about the importance of good quality ingredients and how to find them, and the need to create a good relationship with local fishmongers, butchers and market traders, and the possibilities of growing herbs on windowsills.

His producer recognized that Oliver could put across that cooking was essentially 'sexy', and both the TV and the books, almost for the first time, attracted 'ordinary blokes' into the kitchen. Jamie Oliver enthused that his favourite dishes were 'pukka' (one of his TV programmes was 'Pukka Tukka'), and despite his Essex roots, many of his Italian dishes were indeed pukka, and his enthusiasm and love of Italy and Italian food became infectious.

In *Jamie's Italy*,[23] he mentions an old Tuscan meat dish known as *peposo*, containing a substantial amount of pepper (*pepe* in Italian), which he refers to as 'the famous hunter's peppery beef stew'. My recipe for this comes from a good Florentine friend, Roberto, who lives in Devon.

PEPOSO

Serves 4

600g (1¼lb) stewing beef, cut into 5cm (2in) cubes. Stewing steak or chuck beef will do very well, and if the butcher has a shin bone of veal or beef, that could be thrown in as well.

6 cloves garlic, peeled

2 sprigs fresh rosemary (these could be tied with string so that the leaves do not scatter around)

1–2 bay leaves

3 ripe tomatoes, skinned and roughly chopped, or 2 tbsp tinned tomatoes

1 heaped tbsp freshly ground black pepper

salt to taste

2 large glasses (approx. 300ml or ½ pint) good Chianti wine, such as Poggiopiano, or another robust red

a little meat stock (optional)

4 slices good bread (preferably multigrain, sourdough or Altamura)

Preheat the oven to 150°C (300°F, gas mark 2).

Choose a pan just the right size for all the ingredients. A heavy, enamelled saucepan with a lid (or you can use a thick layer of foil to cover) is ideal, or a terracotta pot would also be excellent.

Put in the chunks of meat and cover with the garlic, rosemary, bay leaves and tomatoes. Add the pepper, and a little salt. Now add the wine, and perhaps a little water to ensure the ingredients are just covered by the liquid. Cover the pan, bring to the boil, and place it in the preheated oven for approximately three hours. After an hour or so, check that the meat is not becoming dry; if it is, just add a little meat stock or hot water.

When ready the meat should be well cooked and slightly soft. Taste and add more salt if necessary.

Toast the bread and spoon the meat and the juices over the slices of toast, and serve.

Nigella Lawson and Anna Del Conte

WHAT IS AUTHENTIC?

It is impossible for me, and tedious even if I could, to list all the TV
programmes dedicated to Italian food, but I shall mention just a few of the
most popular, such as 'Nigella'.

    The glamorous Nigella Lawson graduated in French and Italian at Oxford,
and then became a journalist, but the passion for food and especially for
Italian food must already have been embedded. When she started writing
restaurant reviews for *The Spectator* this became a professional interest. Her
first book, *How to Eat. The pleasures and principles of good food* (1998), was
very well received and Ruth Rogers of The River Café thought the book

was bound to become the staple cookbook for a whole generation. Nigella's approach to food is eminently practical – she frequently refers to personal experience – and her recipes cross a wide range of national boundaries: from British, to French, Italian, Greek, a little Spanish, as well as Jewish, Moroccan, Cambodian and East Asian. As a former contributor to *Vogue*, she is very aware of fashion, and 'chic' is one of her favourite words. Instead of offering a banal, tired recipe for tiramisù,[24] she opts for a chic white tiramisù, which she acknowledges 'bears the mark of Anna del Conte', and 'is far less effort in the kitchen than it looks on the page'. Recipes in her repertoire range from the well-known Piedmontese anchovy and garlic sauce, *bagna cauda*, and a classic *pasta e fagioli* (pasta with beans) to soft and sharp *involtini* inspired more by Greek than Italian flavours. For her 'Italian sausages with lentils' she recommends using proper *genovese* sausages with garlic and basil.[25] So, even if Nigella is an international cook, she acknowledges a marked influence of Italy, and some of her recipes may be defined as a mixture of British and Italian cuisine.

The term 'Britalian' was coined by Anna Del Conte for what she considered hybrid dishes, which originated in Italy but were then transformed to suit British taste. From time to time some people complain about this tendency and discuss what 'genuine' food really is.

Italian trade commission reports at the beginning of the twenty-first century revealed that the fastest growth areas for Italian suppliers were cheese, cured meats, bakery products, balsamic vinegar, specialized olive oils and pasta sauces. Various popular surveys revealed that under-35s in particular were very fond of Italian cuisine. Pasta was still the most purchased Italian product, but cheeses, risotto rice and Italian cured meats were gaining popularity, and the provision of ready-made sauces was certainly on the increase. But how authentic were they?[26] According to Sainsbury's, even if the sale of Italian products was increasing, too much authenticity was not acceptable for most British palates, which were not happy with the high level of acidity in tomatoes and an excessive use of garlic in Italian sauces inspired by southern Italian chefs. The supermarket's spokesman admitted that 'authentic' products available in top delicatessens had a niche market, while large chains opted for more 'acceptable' versions, adopted after studying taste tests carried out with customers.[27]

The controversy is a little unfair, as the same has happened with all ethnic cuisines. A genuine Madras curry or an authentic Chinese dish may be too much for British palates, and the same is happening with Italian food. After all, even in a book by Dorothy Hartley, *Food in England*, published in 1954, we find the following statement:

> English cooking is old-fashioned, because we like it that way. We do enjoy foreign dishes and admire Continental cooks, but when we cook the foreign dishes, the dishes, like the foreigners, become 'naturalized English'.[28]

Only when travelling in Italy can one find truly authentic products, but even then they may not always be of the highest quality. Indeed one should always be wary of claims made about the quality or the origin of individual items. Some labelled as 'artisanal products' may just be produced by large industries. There are excellent vegetables, cheeses and meats produced locally in England and to recognize such products we should refer to trusted and tested retailers.

One TV series which purports to show food and art in their proper context is 'Italy Unpacked', with the chef Giorgio Locatelli and art historian Andrew Graham-Dixon. They visit iconic towns and cities where there are interesting or striking little-known art treasures, as well as gastronomic delights. Every stop ends with Locatelli cooking a local speciality, and frequently shopping is done at market stalls or in small specialized shops.

The first programme shows the two protagonists cooking and eating *tagliatelle al ragù* in Bologna and visiting an *acetaia*, where traditional balsamic vinegar is aged in small wooden barrels. They explore the Renaissance centre of Ferrara, but two of the town's specialities, *cappellacci con la zucca* (pumpkin ravioli) and *salama* or *salamina da sugo* (an intensely flavoured salami with juice, which can only be consumed after a long, careful simmering) don't get a mention. Maybe they were considered 'too authentic' by the programme editors? I was interested to note, however, that on their way to Parma (famed,

of course, for its cheese and cured ham), they stopped near the small town of Zibello, where some of the best *culatello* (literally 'little bum'), is produced. *Culatello* is a cured pork meat that has been made for centuries, and was highly prized by, among others, the composer Giuseppe Verdi and the poet and decadent writer Gabriele D'Annunzio.

I am very partial to the subtle flavour of real, artisanally produced *culatello*, and I naturally wanted to know more about its production, so I went to interview Massimo Spigaroli, who runs a restaurant and a *relais* hotel with his brother, and who produces this sweet and sublime treat in its most authentic form.

Massimo told me the fascinating story of his family, starting with his grandfather who used to work for Verdi, and how, as a child, he was scared by the salami hanging over his cot. He also mentioned that he had been asked by HRH the Prince of Wales to prepare some *culatello* exclusively for his use. The Prince may have discovered this speciality when attending 'Terra Madre' (Mother Earth), a Slow Food event at the University of Gastronomic Science in 2006, in Piedmont, or on one of his other numerous visits to Italy. In the Spigaroli cellars one could spot the names of celebrity chefs, top designers and other famous names attached to individual batches of *culatelli*.

Massimo explained how the best *culatello* is made using only high quality pork, taken from the central muscle of the pig's thigh (the ham), which is boned and cleaned – only a tiny 2 per cent fat in the central part of the meat is allowed. The raw *culatelli* are salted for about ten days, with 3.3 per cent salt to the weight of the individual piece. They are then washed with local white wine and carefully massaged with salt, ground pepper and a little garlic. The meat is then inserted in a pig's bladder or large intestine, and tied with a thick string, in a careful pattern. It is then hung in cellars for a period of 10–12 months, during which time, depending on the climate, it may be necessary to dab each one with a little more wine to avoid it drying too quickly. The subtle smell in Massimo's cellars is a clear indication of this procedure. The preparation of this precious *salume* [any kind of cured meat] takes place between November and February, and it is rumoured that exposure to the thick fog that appears at this time of year is necessary for the curing to be

Mercato Centrale, Florence

wholly successful: no artificial refrigeration in the 'foggy bottoms.'[29] No chemical preservatives are used either (industrial production of *culatelli* uses controlled temperature refrigeration and a small amount of nitrates).

Authentic *culatello*, properly cured according to Massimo Spigaroli's description, is not easy to find outside the Parma region, although I have found it in excellent trattorias in Rome. Even in Italy it is not easily found outside the Emilia-Romagna region, and the *culatello* usually available is mostly commercially produced and hasn't got the refined aroma of the handmade (it's possible it contains some chemical preservatives); a similar, pre-packed version has appeared in at least one mainstream British supermarket.

ALL ABOUT FLAVOUR

More typical Italian ingredients have arrived in the new millennium, helping to sustain the appetite for all things Italian. Take, for example, *burrata*, a creamy type of mozzarella made with buffalo milk, which originated in southern Italy. I had never heard of it before, but when it became popular in food magazines, and some bloggers started enthusing about the 'heavenly, creamy, delicate, fresh Italian cheese that dreams are made of' it became part of the marketing that stimulates the curiosity of customers, and it started appearing on supermarket shelves.

Another product originally produced on a very small scale in southern Italy suddenly became intriguing and exciting in London as well. It was called *'nduja* and I wonder if the unusual name, apparently connected with the French *andouille*, a type of sausage, contributed to its fame. *'Nduja* is a spreadable kind of spicy pork salami which originally was made exclusively for home consumption in some small villages of Calabria, with a considerable amount of local chillis. The international success of this ingredient, hailed as

(facing) Massimo Spigaroli's cellar for *culatello* orders
(overleaf) Cheese on display in Eataly, New York City

a new gustatory experience, has now resulted in an increase in the rearing of pork, and the hot peppers that go with the meat in Calabria are now grown on a much larger scale than ever before.[30]

Other regional specialities are appearing in supermarkets, especially in the area of cured meats and local cheeses. Tuscan *prosciutto* is now sold and branded as *prosciutto del Poggio*,[31] along with Parma ham and *bresaola*, the dry cured beef from Lombardy, and sliced *pancetta*, which, unlike bacon, can be eaten without cooking. Italian cooked ham is also available in most supermarkets, and it is characterized by its special aroma produced by the herbs used in the curing, and the cooking process. One of the most recent products I have spotted in a supermarket is *rigatino affumicato*, which is a typical kind of Tuscan smoked *pancetta*, and I am sure that the word *rigatino* (streaky) is not known to many Italians. For patriotic reasons, I must also mention the appearance on some supermarket shelves of a 'Piacenza platter', with slices of *coppa* and salami.

The attempt to recreate the flavours and products that were until recently found only in Italy is unprecedented, both in the UK and North America. Naturally, the consumer should always be aware of the possible implications of marketing, but always try new products, and seek advice if necessary. Once upon a time it was very frustrating for people returning from trips to Italy who found it impossible to find the flavours and the quality of dishes they had tried in Rome or Venice, or, even more so, in small rural trattorias. No longer. The success of the largely London-based Polpo chain is testament to this. Russell Norman and Richard Beatty opened their first café-bar in Soho in 2009 with the idea of re-creating the flavours and atmosphere of a Venetian *bácaro* (originally a wine shop selling cheap wine). Their philosophy is summed up in the *cichèti* (perhaps from French *chiquet*, 'morsel, small drink') they serve, traditional small dishes to accompany drinks at the bar. These are a kind of modern take on *tapas* with simple and humble 'but always delicious' flavours, and a wide range of ingredients, often Venetian.

In this context I would like to mention an exceptional chef who is a real champion of Italian cuisine in Britain, and in particular of the food I am familiar with, from my home territory.

Chef Angela Hartnett's Italian mother comes from Bardi, in the hills of Parma. After working with Gordon Ramsay (who likes using Italian names for some of his own creations)[32] and in other top restaurants, she opened Murano, and later Café Murano, in St James and Covent Garden. In 2007 she was given an MBE and her restaurant was awarded a Michelin star. In the same year she published her first book: *Cucina: Three Generations of Italian Family Cooking*, celebrating family life and its cooking traditions.[33]

Reading her book, I could smell the distinctive aroma of each dish, and I could share the ritual that accompanied some of them, such as the making of *anolini*, the typical meat ravioli for Christmas. Traditionally, this is a collective experience, in which some members of the family make the pasta, some see to the elaborate filling, while others prepare the special *brodo*, the stock in which they are to be cooked. The children are allowed to arrange the finished ravioli into neat lines on the floured wooden table, so that the little parcels can be easily counted.

The recipes I encountered were very familiar, such as penne bolognese, spaghetti with garlic and *peperoncini* (the Italian term for the tiny hot peppers underlining their 'Italianness') or rigatoni with tomato and *pancetta*. Some dishes were more refined – artichoke and langoustine risotto, crab linguine, lobster spaghetti – as befits a Michelin-starred chef, but most recipes spoke a dialect very similar to my own. Angela Hartnett's cuisine derives largely from her Italian maternal grandmother, and some recipes have been passed down through generations of women.

Many of her desserts are also extremely familiar, none more so than her almond cake. This is something I am very fond of, and I have made it myself on various occasions, using this recipe of my mother's (Hartnett's version is slightly different, and uses self-raising flour and lemon zest). Its execution is quite simple:

ALMOND CAKE

Serves 4–6

300g (11oz) almonds. Whole ones with their skin, very finely chopped, will provide the best result, but ready-ground almonds can be used
6 organic/free range eggs (the freshest possible), separated
150–180g (5–6oz) caster sugar (my mother would use 180g but I found this slightly too sweet).

Heat the oven to 160°C (320°F, gas mark 3).

Grease a 23cm (9in) cake tin, and add some sugar (or flour), shake the tin and remove excess. This will help the removal of the baked cake.

If using whole almonds, put them through an electric blender until fairly smooth.

Whisk the egg yolks in a large bowl with the sugar, either by hand using a wooden spoon, or with an electric blender, until the mixture is quite smooth and the sugar is no longer grainy. The colour should be pale yellow.

In a separate bowl, whisk the egg whites well until they can form standing peaks.

Using a large metal spoon or a balloon whisk, slowly turn the beaten whites into the yolk and sugar mixture, then gently add the almonds a tablespoon at a time.

Pour the mixture into the greased cake tin. Bake in the pre-heated oven for about 40 minutes. When the cake has a light brown crust it should be ready, but you can check by inserting a wooden skewer into the cake, and if it emerges fairly dry, the cake is ready.

Leave to rest and when cool, carefully transfer on to a plate. It can be eaten the day after, and even after a couple of days any leftover cake will still be excellent.

The success of Italian food in Britain seems unstoppable, and restaurants with Italian names are appearing all over the place. The most recent one I have found is in London's Barbican, named Osteria ('tavern', which seems a bit of a misnomer), in which the Michelin-starred chef Anthony Demetre presents a menu featuring a range of Italian regional classics from all over the country, paired with an innovative Italian wine list. But places like Trullo in Islington, and the connected Padella ('frying pan'), south of the river, have attracted the attention of food critics. Trullo offers some of the best interpretations of Italian food, made by top-class British chefs. As a starter you can have *scorzonera*, an intriguing long root very similar to salsify, lightly cooked with cheese, or sample some vegetables with a sprinkling of *ricotta salata*. Their pappardelle with beef shin ragù is full of flavour, the sauce is just right, and the amount of grated Parmesan enhances the whole. And menus are changing daily. Padella has a relatively small menu, and pasta is at the centre of it, but many people feel that it would be worth trying everything, since it all looks inviting and potentially exciting.

There are, of course, a very large number of traditional and more innovative Italian restaurants in London and across the country, some of them of very high quality, but if I had to choose one that represents the 'essence of Italian food', I would go for Jacob Kenedy's Bocca di Lupo in Soho. (The name translates as 'wolf's mouth', but there is also a nod to the expression *In bocca al lupo*, with which you might wish someone good luck.) Opened in 2009, it has been a great success because of the variety of regional Italian food on offer, in small or larger portions, so that you can sample whatever looks intriguing or attractive. Jay Rayner, reviewing the restaurant, said that the menu looks more like a wine list, and you can imagine visiting Lombardy with a good risotto, or Tuscany with some pecorino, Lazio with some spaghetti amatriciana, or even artichokes in the Jewish fashion (*carciofi alla giudía*), Calabria with spicy *'nduja* and so on.

More and more people seem to be keen to buy genuine, good quality Italian products, and the large markets known as Eataly (from Eat + Italy) have sprung up in a number of cities, where they occupy renovated buildings that have long lain empty. Their motto is 'eat, shop and learn', and they feature an array of cafés, counters, restaurants and cooking schools. From its origins in a former Vermouth factory in Turin, Eataly has gone global, opening in New York, Boston, Chicago and more recently in Los Angeles. Russia and China seem to be future destinations. In London, the connected Mercato Metropolitano opened in 2016, offering a huge variety of quality products, as well as a specialized wine shop, conjuring up food markets in Milan or Turin.

It seems we have come a long way from the little bottle of refined olive oil for medicinal purposes. Now we are distinguishing between single-estate Tuscan extra virgin, Lucca v. Siena, Ligurian oil v. light Garda, or complex, intense Apulian, Calabrian, Sicilian and Sardinian olive oils. Oil tasting is no longer a weird concept. And the oil has acquired its own acronym: EVO, which at first puzzled me in some recipes. It stands, of course, for extra virgin olive oil. Palates have become more discerning.

The Romans, and the members of the varied ethnic groups that formed their ranks, started the trend of importing good olives and olive oil, good food and good wine from the continent, but then they learnt to brew beer, grow plants and breed cattle in Britain, sharing their crops with the locals. Later, generations of immigrants came from various parts of Italy to work in London, Edinburgh and Glasgow as well as Manchester, Birmingham, Bedford and Cardiff. They brought their skills to contribute to the improvement of life in a community that at times may have seemed hostile, but was able to appreciate their hard work and positive contribution to the common good. As a mayor of Edinburgh once put it: 'The Italians have come to look for a better life and they have taught us a better way of living.' A huge number of immigrants have worked in cafés, in restaurants, in hotels, and used their contacts to import new foods, and to suggest new experiences, to the joy of British palates. The origin of the word *companion* is in the sharing of food (bread, in this case, *panis* in Latin) with another human being.

I still believe that the EU, with all its shortcomings, represents a very positive contribution to the principles of tolerance, reason and understanding that I have found in all the parts of Britain where I have worked and lived. I have tried to inculcate these same principles to thousands of students over the years.

Maybe at some point in the future Italian food will be absorbed into the culinary tradition of the UK, and the British may become sated with it, but so far there is no sign of any diminution in the craving for quality Italian food, properly cooked and at decent prices. And to see young farmers and growers trying to rediscover local traditions, learn new techniques and contribute to the education of taste is truly inspiring.

GLOSSARY

Names in **bold** indicate an independent entry

Abbacchio: roast lamb (mainly in Rome).

Acciughe: anchovies.

Aceto (di vino rosso/bianco): (red/white) wine vinegar; aceto balsamico: balsamic vinegar.

Acquacotta: one of the many simple soups based on vegetables, oil, stale bread and eggs. Lit. 'cooked water'.

Amatriciana, also *matriciana*: from the town of Amatrice in Latium. Sauce (usually for *pasta all'amatriciana*) made with olive oil, onion, *guanciale* and tomato, with a little *peperoncino*.

Anguria: watermelon (known as *cocomero* in Tuscany).

Anolini: circular ravioli filled with *stracotto* meat, Parmesan and spices, found in Piacenza and Parma.

Arborio: type of rice for risotto.

Arugula: see *Rucola*.

Bagna cauda, also spelt *bagna caôda*: Piedmontese dipping hot sauce, made with anchovies, garlic and butter.

Bologna: usually short for Bologna sausage, a type of **mortadella**.

Borlotti: type of freckled red-brown beans (cranberry beans in the USA), usually dried, but available fresh in the summer in Italy.

Bottarga: salted and preserved fish (especially mullet) roe.

Bresaola: select cuts of beef cured with salt and spices, usually finely sliced. Originally from the Lombard valley, Valtellina.

Brodo: broth or stock. Most commonly *di carne* (meat), *di pollo* (chicken), *vegetale* (vegetable). The diminutive, *brodetto*, is usually a thin soup or reduced stock.

Bruschetta: a slice of toast with tomato, garlic, olive oil, or a variety of toppings, such as fried chicken livers, beans, spinach or mushrooms. Syn. *crostino*.

Bucatini: a variety of large spaghetti.

Budino: a general word for 'pudding' but may refer to a soft, jelly-like sweet.

Burrata: soft mozzarella.

Cacciatori/cacciatorini: small salami, usually made with pork or wild boar, traditionally carried by hunters for their lunch. Lit. 'hunters', 'small hunters'.

Caciocavallo: an ancient cheese from southern Italy made with milk from semi-wild cows (*Podolica* breed), which graze on wild herbs. Lit. 'cheese-horse'.

Calzone: a type of pizza folded over and with a variety of fillings. Lit. 'trousers'.

Cannellini: white beans from Tuscany.

Cannelloni: large tubes of pasta filled with ricotta and spinach, or many other fillings, usually baked.

Cannoli: a Sicilian pastry roll, deep fried and filled with sweet **ricotta**.

Cappellacci: a kind of **ravioli**, mainly from Ferrara. Lit. 'rickety hats'.

Cappelletti: small **ravioli**, similar to tortellini, but typical of Romagna. Lit. 'dainty hats', 'helmets'.

Carbonara: pasta (usually **spaghetti, bucatini, penne**) in a sauce made with *guanciale*, whole egg and pecorino cheese. No cream is used in the Roman original version.

Carciofo: artichoke. Usually prepared *alla giudía*, in the Jewish fashion (deep fried), or *alla romana*: in the Roman fashion (boiled).

Carciofini: small artichokes, usually cooked in acidulated water and preserved in olive oil.

Cardo: cardoon, giant thistle similar to artichoke.

Carnaroli: Lombard rice suitable for risotto.

Carpaccio: wafer-thin slices of raw beef fillet, served with olive oil, lemon juice and slivers of Parmesan. The name was invented by Arrigo Cipriani at Harry's Bar in Venice, around 1964, during an exhibition dedicated to the Venetian Renaissance painter Vittore Carpaccio.

Castelfranco: a type of speckled **radicchio** from the Veneto region.

Cavolo nero: black kale.

Cenci: pasta fritters.

Ciabatta: new type of bread produced in the 1980s to look like traditional Tuscan bread.

Colatura di alici: a thin sauce made with salt sardines. See p. 15.

Conchiglie: type of pasta shaped like shells.

Coppa: cured pork meat from the neck and loin of the pig. Typical of Parma and Piacenza. The southern *capocollo* is similar.

Crostino: see **Bruschetta**.

Culatello: one of the most highly prized types of cured pork: see p. 188.

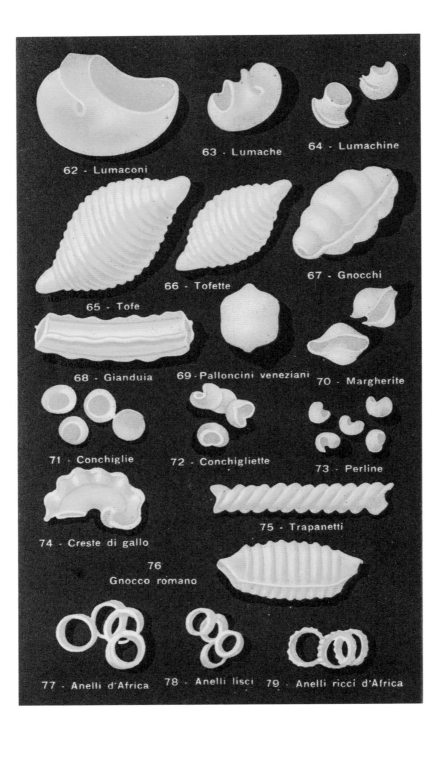

62 - Lumaconi

63 - Lumache

64 - Lumachine

65 - Tofe

66 - Tofette

67 - Gnocchi

68 - Gianduia

69 - Palloncini veneziani

70 - Margherite

71 - Conchiglie

72 - Conchigliette

73 - Perline

74 - Creste di gallo

75 - Trapanetti

76
Gnocco romano

77 - Anelli d'Africa

78 - Anelli lisci

79 - Anelli ricci d'Africa

Ditali: type of small pasta, very short macaroni. Lit. 'thimbles'.

Dolce: sweet, dessert or cake.

Fagioli: beans.

Farfalle: type of pasta shaped like bow ties (in Italian *farfalle* is also butterflies).

Fettuccine: ribbons of pasta similar to **tagliatelle**.

Fiori di zucca/zucchini fritti: fried pumpkin/courgette flowers. See p. 100.

Focaccia: yeasted bread dough often mixed with oil, onions and herbs and salt, similar to pizza.

Frittata: omelette.

Frittelle (di borraggine, di ceci): fritters (of borage, chickpeas) etc.

Fritto misto: 'mixed fry', which can be fish and seafood fried crisp, or deep fried vegetables in batter.

Frutti di mare: seafood.

Funghi: mushrooms. *Funghi secchi* (dried mushrooms); *funghi ripieni* (stuffed mushrooms). *Funghi trifolati* are fried with chopped parsley and garlic.

Fusilli: type of pasta, twisted like a corkscrew.

Garganelli: type of pasta made from a small square of thin dough.

Giardiniera: vegetables, such as carrots, pimento, onions, fennel, turnip preserved in vinegar, and served with olive oil.

Gnocchi: small dumplings. Variations include *gnocchi di patate* (potato), *gnocchi verdi* (spinach), *gnocchi alla romana* (Roman, usually made with semolina). *Gnocchetti sardi* (or *malloreddus* in Sardinian) are small Sardinian gnocchi, usually served with tomato sauce.

Gnudi: ravioli without pasta. See p. 29.

Grana: a type of less expensive **Parmigiano**, although sometimes it refers to Parmesan itself. Grana padano is a Parmesan-type cheese produced outside the area of Parmigiano Reggiano.

Grappa: spirit distilled from grapes or grape dregs.

Gremolata: a fine mix of lemon zest, chopped parsley and garlic, sprinkled over some dishes at the end of cooking.

Guanciale: cured pork jowl.

Involtini: rolls of thin slices of veal or beef.

Lardo: pork back fat.

Lasagne: large strips of pasta layered with meat or other sauce and béchamel.

Linguine: type of pasta in narrow strips.

Lumache: snails; also pasta shaped like snail shells. Diminutive: *lumachine*.

Maccheroni: the original, Italian spelling of 'macaroni'.

Maltagliati: small strips of fresh pasta.

Maniche: short pasta shape. Lit: 'sleeves'.

Midollo: bone marrow.

Minestra: soup to which some type of pasta is usually added.

Mortadella: a characteristically deep pink-coloured sausage. The best type is made from finely minced pork with a proportion of *lardo* and spices. It is usually slowly steamed before reaching the shops.

Mozzarella: soft cheese from buffalo milk, if made with cow milk it is usually called 'fior di latte'.

'Nduja: a very spicy, spreadable salami from Calabria.

Olio d'oliva extra vergine: extra virgin olive oil (sometimes called *olio EVO*), first cold-pressed pure olive oil.

Oliva (verde/nera): olive (green/black); paté d'olive: olive pâté (tapenade). Olive ascolane: big olives from Ascoli Piceno, usually filled with meat, anchovies, and deep fried.

Orecchiette: type of pasta from Apulia. Lit. 'little ears'.

Orzo: barley. Also a shape of small pasta, usually added to soups.

Osso buco: slow-cooked veal shin. See p. 30.

Pancetta: cured pork belly, similar to bacon but large and rolled; *pancetta* can be sliced and eaten after curing.

Pandoro: Christmas cake, mainly from Milan, it has no candied fruit, unlike *panettone*.

Panettone: typical Christmas cake from Milan, usually with sultanas and candied fruit.

Panforte: a dense medieval cake, used especially at Christmas in Siena, made with lots of dried fruit, almonds, and sugar.

Panna cotta: sweet made with cooked cream, sugar and vanilla.

Pappardelle: type of broad pasta ribbons, larger than tagliatelle.

Parmigiano: Parmesan cheese. Parmigiano Reggiano is the certified variety.

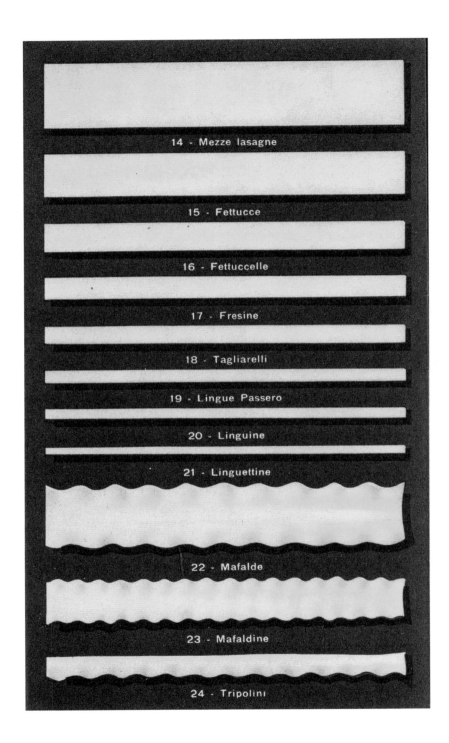

14 - Mezze lasagne

15 - Fettucce

16 - Fettuccelle

17 - Fresine

18 - Tagliarelli

19 - Lingue Passero

20 - Linguine

21 - Linguettine

22 - Mafalde

23 - Mafaldine

24 - Tripolini

Passatelli: typical *minestra* from Romagna, made with eggs, breadcrumbs and Parmesan, passed through a coarse ricer, and cooked in a good broth.

Pastina per brodo: small pasta, such as *orzo, stelline, lumachine*, which is cooked rapidly in broth.

Pecorino: hard cheese made with ewe's milk. It can be fresh or mature (*stagionato*), and the three main areas of production are Tuscany (*pecorino toscano*), Rome and Lazio (*pecorino romano*) and Sardinia (*pecorino sardo*).

Penne: type of short pasta. Lit. 'pen nib'.

Peperoncino: chilli pepper.

Peposo: a peppery Tuscan stew. See p. 182.

Pesto: sauce, originally from Genoa, made with basil, garlic, pine nuts, Parmesan or **pecorino** cheese and extra virgin olive oil.

Piadina: flat bread, mainly found in Romagna (Rimini, Forlì areas).

Piccata: escalope, usually veal.

Pinzimonio: crudités (celery, carrots, artichokes, fennel, spring onion etc.) eaten raw with extra virgin olive oil, salt and pepper.

Polpette: meatballs or rissoles. *Polpettone* is a meat loaf.

Pomodoro: tomato.

Porcini: *Boletus edulis* and similar species of mushroom.

Portulaca: purslane, usually picked from the wild.

Prezzemolo: parsley. Flat-leaf parsley is the only variety in Italy.

Prosciutto: ham. *Prosciutto crudo*: raw ham from cured pork haunches; *prosciutto cotto*: ham cooked with herbs; *prosciutto arrosto*: roast ham; *prosciutto di Parma*: pork ham cured in the hills of Parma.

Puttanesca: sauce with olives, aubergines, garlic and chilli.

Radicchio: type of chicory, usually red. The prime radicchio-growing area is Treviso, so *trevisano* is a type of radicchio.

Ragù: meat sauce. *Ragù alla bolognese*: Bolognese sauce (*soffritto* plus minced beef and pork); *ragù alla napoletana*: Neapolitan sauce (with tomato and larger pieces of beef).

Ravioli: pasta stuffed with an enormous variety of fillings: ricotta, cheese, seafood, mushrooms, vegetables etc.

Ribollita: a type of Tuscan, especially Florentine, minestrone. See p. 180.

Ricotta: a kind of low-fat cheese obtained by re-heating the whey. Lit. 'cooked again'.

Rigatoni: type of tubular, ridged pasta.

Rucola: rocket. A southern variation, *arugula*, is used in the USA.

Salame cotto: cooked, i.e. boiled salami.

Salama da sugo: very intensely flavoured salami that has to be simmered for about three hours. A Ferrarese speciality.

Salmì: from French *salmis*, but in fact more similar to *civet*, a kind of stew mainly of game, typically hare or pheasant.

Salsa: sauce. Common types include *verde* (green, made with parsley), *di pomodoro* (tomato) and *di noci* (walnut).

Saltimbocca: small veal escalope fried with **prosciutto**, cheese and sage. Originally from Rome. Lit. 'jump in the mouth'.

Salumi: cured meats, mainly pork, such as *prosciutto*, *bresaola*, *coppa*, **mortadella**. *pancetta*, salami.

Sambuca: liqueur based on infusion of dill and star anise with elderflowers.

Scorzonera: black salsify.

Semifreddo: dessert similar to ice-cream, usually embellished with sponge and liqueurs.

Semola: durum wheat flour, semolina.

Sfoglia: thin sheet of pasta.

Soffritto: chopped onion, carrot and celery fried in olive oil or butter. The basis of many sauces and preparations.

Spaghetti: a basic shape of pasta, larger than **vermicelli**. It only became more common than macaroni towards the end of the nineteenth century.

Spongata: a traditional fruit cake, mainly made at Christmas in the region around Parma.

Stracotto: meat slowly braised with wine and herbs. Lit. 'extra cooked'.

Strangolapreti: type of pasta or dumplings. Lit. 'priest-strangler'. Many regional variations include *strozzapreti*, *strangozzi*, *strangolaprèvete* and *strangugliaprieviti* (in Calabria).

Stufato: stew.

Sùgoli: grape must jellies. See p. 62.

Tagliatelle: a basic, ribbon-shaped pasta.

Taglierini: thin strips of pasta, especially home made.

Tajarin al tartufo: thin strips of pasta with truffle, from Piedmont.

Tartina: thin slice of bread with various toppings.

Tartufo, tartufato: truffle, truffled.

Timballo: timbale. See p. 111.

Tiramisù: a rich, creamy dessert flavoured with coffee and chocolate, invented in the 1980s in the Veneto region. Lit. 'pick-me-up'.

Topinambur: Jerusalem artichoke.

Torta: cake. Comes in many varieties, including *alle mandorle* (almond). *Torta pasqualina* was originally a vegetable cake made at Easter (Pasqua) in Genoa.

Tortelli: type of ravioli.

Trenette: type of pasta typical of Genoa.

Trippa: tripe.

Trofie: short pasta shape, from Liguria.

Vermicelli: thin, long pasta. Lit. 'little worms'.

Vin santo: Tuscan wine, mainly dessert wine.

Vitello: veal. *Vitello tonnato* is veal escalope in a soft tuna-based sauce.

Zabaglione: creamy dessert made with eggs, marsala and sugar.

Zucca: pumpkin.

Zucchini: courgettes.

Zuppa: soup. Most common soups include *di verdure* (vegetable), *di funghi* (mushroom), *di pesce* (fish).

Zuppa inglese: Italian version of a trifle.

NOTES

1. HOW IT ALL STARTED

1 The culinary use of olive oil was promoted only in the 1950s by the British cookery writer Elizabeth David. For Mrs Beeton's opinion see page 84 [Chapter 3].

2 Julius Caesar, *The Gallic War*, ed. Henry J. Edwards, Harvard University Press, Cambridge, MA and London, 1917, bk. V, pp. 250–51.

3 *A Companion to Roman Britain* ed. Malcolm Todd. Blackwell Reference Online. [http://www.blackwellreference.com/subscriber/book. html?id=g9780631218234_9780631218234, accessed 30 May 2018.] Chapter 1 by Barry Cunliffe.

4 Barrie E. Juniper and David J. Mabberley, *The Story of the Apple*, Timber Press, Portland, OR, 2006.

5 Pliny, *Natural History*, ed. H. Rackham, Heinemann and Harvard University Press, London and Cambridge, MA, 1945, bk XV, pp. 358–9. It is likely that wild cherries had reached Italy long before Lucullus. See Enrico Carnevale Schianca, *La cucina medievale. Lessico, storia, preparazioni*, Olschki, Florence, 2011, p. 152.

6 Cabbages were grown at Fishbourne in West Sussex. Carrots, radishes, parsnips and turnips are known to have been eaten and probably grown at Silchester in Hampshire. See Joan P. Alcock, *Food in Roman Britain*, Tempus, Stroud, 2001, pp. 63–5, and Colleen Cummings, *Food and Society in Late Roman Britain: Determining Dietary Patterns Using Stable Isotopes Analysis*, D. Phil. thesis, University of Oxford, 2008, pp. 89–91. See also E. Carnevale Schianca, *La cucina medievale* pp. 152–3.

7 Rose Gray and Ruth Rogers, *The River Café Cook Book*, Ebury Press, London, 1995, p. 9.

8 Marcus Porcius Cato, *On Agriculture*, William Davis Hooper and Harrison Boyd (eds), Harvard University Press and Heinemann, Cambridge, MA and London, 1979, pp. 140–41.

9 Cummings, *Food and Society in Late Roman Britain*, pp. 61–3.

10 Robert I. Curtis, *Garum and Salsamenta: Production and Commerce in Materia Medica*, Brill, Leiden, 1991.

11 Christopher Grocock and Sally Grainger (eds), *Apicius*. A critical edition with an introduction and an English translation of the Latin recipe text, Prospect Books, London 2006, Appendix 4: 'Excursus on *garum* and *liquamen*,' pp. 373–87. See also Sally Grainger, *Cooking Apicius*, Prospect Books, London, 2006, pp. 27–9, David Downie 'A Roman Anchovy's Tale', *Gastronomica*, vol. 3, No. 2 (Spring 2003), pp. 25–8 and Arthur Schwartz, *Naples at Table*, Harper Collins, New York, 1998, pp. 16–18.

12 Cummings, *Food and Society in Late Roman Britain*, p. 100.

13 Alan K. Bowman, *Life and Letters on the Roman Frontier. Vindolanda and its People*, British Museum, London, 1994, p. 74.

14 The date is given as 11 September, the year is unknown, but probably around 130 CE. See Bowman, *Life and Letters on the Roman Frontier*, p. 57.

15 In English *tourte* is mentioned in 1417 as a bread made of unsifted flour. See William Edward Mead, *The English Medieval Feast*, Allen & Unwin, London, 1967, p. 40.

16 Sally Grainger, *Cooking Apicius*, p. 117.

17 Ibid., p. 56.

18 Ann Hagen, *Anglo-Saxon Food and Drink: Production, Processing, Distribution and Consumption*, Anglo-Saxon Books, Hockwold cum Wilton, 2006.

19 Diana Webb, *Pilgrims and Pilgrimage in the Medieval West*, I. B. Tauris, London and New York, 1999, pp. 18–19, 33–4.

20 *Bede's Ecclesiastical History of the English People*, Bertram Colgrave and Roger A. B. Mynors (eds), Clarendon Press, Oxford, 1969, pp. 142–3.

21 Alban Gautier, *Le festin dans l'Angleterre Anglo-Saxonne (Ve–XIe siècles)*, Presses Universitaires de Rennes, 2006.

22 Clarissa Dickson Wright, *A History of English Food*, Random House, London, 2011, p. 43.

23 This was much to the annoyance of numerous English customers, such as the anonymous author of a fifteenth-century *Libelle* who would have liked the foreign ships banned from English waters. See Jack Turner, *Spice. The History of a Temptation*, Harper Perennial, London, 2005, p. 329.

24 Bruno Laurioux, 'Spices in the Medieval Diet. A New Approach', in *Food & Foodways: Explorations in the History and Culture of Human Nourishment*, vol. 1, no. 1, 1985, pp. 43–75.

25 Toby Peterson, 'The Arab influence on Western European Cooking', *Journal of Medieval History*, v. 6, no. 3 (1980), pp. 317–41.

26 Anna Martellotti, 'Haggis-Pudding', *Petits Propos Culinaires*, 107, January 2017, pp. 29–37, with reference to her edition of the *Liber de ferculis*. See also A. Martellotti, *I ricettari di Federico II*, L. Olschki, Florence, 2005.

27 *Curye on Inglysch. English Culinary Manuscripts of the Fourteenth Century (Including the Forme of Cury)*, Constance B. Hieatt and Sharon Butler (eds), Oxford University Press, London, 1985.

28 Bruno Laurioux, 'Spices in the Medieval Diet. A New Approach', pp. 43–75: 54, Table 3. Jean-Louis Flandrin, 'Brouets, potages et bouillons', *Médiévales*, 5, 1983, pp. 5–13: 10.

29 Rice flour was also used as a thickener of sauces. C. Anne Wilson, *Food and Drink in Britain*, Penguin Books, Harmondsworth, 1976, p. 183.

30 Franco La Cecla, *Pasta and Pizza*, Prickly Paradigm Press, 2007, p. 60: 'Whatever the facts may be, the story was repeated in the *Macaroni Journal* in 1928 where a sailor on Marco Polo's voyage named "Spaghetti" gained possession of directions for making pasta in Cathay.' For the reference to the Sicilian pasta factory, see John Dickie, *Delizia! The Epic History of the Italians and Their Food*, Sceptre, London, 2007, pp. 22–3. See also Silvano Serventi and Françoise Sabban, *Pasta: the Story of a Universal Food*, Columbia University Press, New York and Chichester, 2002.

31 E. Carnevale Schianca, *La cucina medievale*, pp. 680–82.

32 Around 1350 the greatest medieval storyteller, Giovanni Boccaccio (1313–1375) will mention many dishes in his *Decameron*, including macaroni and ravioli, to which butter and grated Parmesan were added.

33 Although Chaucer was well acquainted with Boccaccio's works, he never mentioned him, even if he dedicated some passages of his *Canterbury Tales* to a London cook. *The Works of Geoffrey Chaucer*, Fred N. Robinson (ed.), Oxford University Press, London, 1957: 'General Prologue', pp. 20–21 and 'The Cook's Prologue', p. 60. See also Constance B. Hieatt, 'A Cook of 14th-Century London: Chaucer's Hogge of Ware', in *Cooks and Other People*. Proceedings of

the Oxford Symposium on Food and Cookery, 1995, pp. 138–43.

34 Massimo Montanari, *Alimentazione e cultura nel Medioevo*, Laterza, Bari, 1988, p. 167.

35 *Cury*, *Curye* means 'cookery, kitchen'; it derives from an Old French word, *keu* 'cook', *keuerie* 'cookery', connected to the Latin *cocus* 'cook'. The collection is also referred to as *Forme of Cury*.

36 *Libro della cucina del sec. XIV*, Commissione per i Testi di Lingua, Bologna, 1968 [repr. of 1863 edition], p. 77. Later in Italy, cooks produced a type of even meatier lasagne. Instead of strips of pasta, the skin of hens or capons was used. Capons, neutered cockerels, were used for centuries in cooking, on account of their delicate, fatty meat.

37 *Curye on Inglysch*, p. 108.

38 'One might be tempted to say that Italian recipes travelled almost as far as Italian merchants and tradesmen.' Terence Scully, *The Art of Cookery in the Middle Ages*, The Boydell Press, Woodbridge, 1995, p. 226.

39 See also Constance B. Hieatt, 'Milk: Almond vs. Cow in Medieval English Courtly Cookery', Oxford Symposium on Food & Cookery, 1987 *Taste*, ed. Tom Jaine, Prospect Books, London, 1988, pp. 70–73.

40 *Curye on Inglysch*, p. 118. For variants, such as *ravioles* [of spiced pork], see Peter Brears, *Cooking and Dining in Medieval England*, Prospect Books, Totnes, 2008, p. 282.

41 Clifford A. Wright, 'Cucina arabo-sicula and Maccharruni' in *Al-Masāq: studia arabo-islamica mediterranea*, vol. 9, 1996–7, pp. 151–77.

42 Massimo Montanari, *Il sugo della storia*, Laterza, Bari, 2016, pp. 12–13, maintains that, although *tortelli* (of which *tortelletti* is a diminutive) is now a synonym of *ravioli* in Italian, in the Middle Ages *tortelli* referred to the 'twisted' pasta casings to be filled. See also Maguelonne Toussaint-Samat, 'Une recette du XVe siècle': *De modo faciendis Tortellos assisianos*, in *Médiévales*, No. 5, 1983, pp. 94–5.

43 In *Libro della cucina*, p. 37, there is a recipe for *guanti* ('gloves') or *ravioli*, made with mashed chickpeas and fried in pork fat or oil, and another for *tortelli*, on p. 78.

44 Salimbene de Adam, *Cronica*, ed. Ferdinando Bernini, Laterza, Bari, 1942, vol. 2, p. 264.

45 Heston Blumenthal, *Historic Heston*, Bloomsbury, London, 2013, pp. 34–8, considers the dish cooked at the Plantagenet court as 'effectively a baked cheesecake'. See also E. Carnevale Schianca, *La cucina medievale*, pp. 591–2.

46 Bartolomeo Sacchi, known as Platina from the Latin name of his home town, Piàdena near Cremona, wrote a treatise in Latin, entitled *De Honesta Voluptate et Valetudine*, around 1467. *Platina, on Right Pleasure and Good Health: a Critical Edition and Translation of 'De Honesta Voluptate et Valetudine'*, ed. Mary Ella Milham, Medieval & Renaissance Texts & Studies, Tempe, AZ, 1998, but the new edition with the Latin and Italian texts and full commentary is superior: *De honesta voluptate et valetudine. Un trattato sui piaceri della tavola e la buona salute*, ed. Enrico Carnevale Schianca, Olschki, Florence, 2015.

47 Now recognized as Martino Rossi, see *The Art of Cooking. The First Modern Cookery Book Composed by the Eminent Maestro Martino of Como*, Luigi Ballerini, Jeremy Parzen and Stefania Barzini (eds), University of California Press, Berkeley, 2005; the recipe for the elderflower *torte* is on p. 82.

48 Claudio Benporat, *Cucina italiana del quattrocento*, Olschki, Florence, 1996, p. 201.

49 *Curye on Inglysch*, pp. 71–2, p. 101, p. 125.

50 Giovanni Boccaccio, *Decameron*, Day 8, third tale, ed. Vittore Branca, Mondadori, Milan, 1976, p. 682.

2. EARLY ENGLISH TRAVELLERS TO ITALY

1   The idea of a purgatory was created in the thirteenth century. At the second Council of Lyon in 1274, purgatory was put on the books, and in the Council of Trent it was given a definite status. See Jacques Le Goff, *The Birth of Purgatory*, Scolar Press, London, 1984.

2   An example is the anonymous *Informac[i]on for pylgrymes vnto the Holy Londe*, [Wynkyn de Word, London, 1500?], mainly in English but with some sections in Latin. It provides distances in miles between various towns, starting with a chapter from Calais to Rome via France. Further on there is information on the pilgrimage to the holy sepulcher 'by the Duche waye', with sections on the exchange value of the various currencies, from England to Rome and Venice.

3   *The Book of Margery Kempe. The Text from the Unique Ms. Owned by Colonel W. Butler-Bowdon*, Sanford Brown Meech and Hope Emily Allen (eds), Early English Text Society, Rochester, NY, and Woodbridge, 1997.

4   Anthony Goodman, *Margery Kempe and Her World*, Longman, Harlow, 2002.

5   See also Laura Pinnavaia, *The Italian Borrowings in the Oxford English Dictionary: a Lexicographical, Linguistic and Cultural Analysis*, Bulzoni, Rome, 2001.

6   *Two Renaissance Book Hunters: the Letters of Poggius Bracciolini to Nicolaus de Niccolis*; translated from the Latin and annotated by Phyllis Walter Goodhart Gordan, Columbia University Press, New York, 1991, p. 111. Christopher S. Celenza, *Renaissance Humanism and the Papal Curia: Lapo da Castiglionchio the Younger, De curiae commodis*, University of Michigan Press, Ann Arbor, 1999, esp. section VII, pp. 29–31.

7   As suggested by Gillian Riley, 'Platina, Martino and Their Circle', in *Cooks & Other People. Proceedings of the Oxford Symposium on Food and Cookery 1995*, ed. Harlan Walker, Prospect Books, Totnes, 1996, pp. 214–19. These imported recipes might have represented a kind of 'new cuisine' which called for a simplification, a 'purification' of the old cuisine, inspired by the Romans. Humanist ideas influenced by classical literature were common in higher-class circles in central Italy in the fifteenth century. This was the time when learned popes such as Nicholas V, Pius II and Sixtus IV dominated Rome, and therefore Platina, as head of the Vatican Library, can be seen as the precursor of 'new ideas' borrowed from his friend Martino. See also Bruno Laurioux, *Gastronomie, humanisme et société à Rome au milieu du XVe siècle: autour du De honesta voluptate de Platina*, Edizioni Galluzzo-SISMEL, Florence, 2006.

8   *The Pylgrymage of Sir Richard Guylforde to the Holy Land, A.D. 1506: from a Copy Believed to Be Unique, from the Press of Richard Pynson*, ed. Henry Ellis, Camden Society, London, 1851.

9   *Ye Oldest Diarie of Englysshe Travell Being the Hitherto Unpublished Narrative of the Pilgrimage of Sir Richard Torkington to Jerusalem in 1517*, ed. William J. Loftie, Fiel & Tuer, London, 1884.

10   Ibid., p. 5.

11   Some eighteenth-century recipes for the making of sausages and salami can be found in Piacenza, Biblioteca Comunale, MS. Comun. 556, fols 3v–4r.

12   Torkington, *Ye oldest diarie*, p. 7.

13   Ibid., pp. 12–13.

14   Elizabeth Lane Furdell, 'Boorde, Andrew (*c.*1490–1549)', in *Oxford Dictionary of National Biography*, Oxford University Press, 2004; online edn, [http://ezproxy-prd.bodleian.ox.ac.uk:2167/view/article/2870, accessed 22 Nov 2017].

15   Andrew Borde, *Gli itinerari d'Europa. (The Introduction of Knowledge)*, ed. Maria Palermo Concolato, Liguori, Napoli, 1992.

16   The manuscript is dated *c.*1450, but it was printed in 1502. Michele Savonarola, *Libreto de*

tutte le cosse che se magnano; un'opera di dietetica del sec. XV, ed. Jane Nysted, Almqvist & Wiskell International, Stockholm, 1988.

17 Scappi (*c*.1500–1577) was chef to no fewer than six popes, and his monumental work, *Opera di Bartolomeo Scappi, mastro dell'arte del cucinare, divisa in sei libri*, contained about 1,000 recipes. It is now available in English: *The Opera of Bartolomeo Scappi (1570): the Art and Craft of a Master Cook,* ed. Terence Scully, University of Toronto Press, Toronto and London, 2008.

18 William Thomas, *Principal Rules of the Italian Grammer: with a Dictionarie for the Better Vunderstandynge of Boccacce, Petrarcha and Dante*, [Thomas Powell], London, 1562. For further information on William Thomas see Edward Chaney, *The Evolution of the Grand Tour. Anglo-Italian Cultural Relations Since the Renaissance*, Frank Cass, London, 1998, pp. 70–6.

19 These include John Lyly (1554?–1606) and his work *Euphues. The Anatomy of Wit*, Gabriel Cawood, London [1578]. See also Sara Warneke, *Images of the Educational Traveller in Early Modern England*, Brill, Leiden,1995.

20 Thomas Nash, *The Works of Thomas Nashe*, Ronald Brunlees McKerrow and Frank Percy Wilson (eds), Blackwell, Oxford, 1958, 5 vols, vol. 2, p. 301.

21 Thomas Hoby, 'The Travels and Life of Sir Thomas Hoby Kt. of Bisham Abbey, Written by Himself, 1547–64', ed. Edgar Powell, in *The Camden Miscellany*, vol. 10, pp. v–xxiv and pp. 1–144.

22 Hoby, 'The Travels and Life', p. 37.

23 Ibid., pp. 29–30.

24 Ibid., p. 29.

25 Dante Alighieri, *Commedia*, Mondadori, Milan, 1994, Purgatorio, canto XXIV, vv. 21–4. See also Marco Lisi, *Sulle tracce della Vernaccia dal XIII al XXI secolo*, Nuova Immagine, Siena, 2013.

26 Especially the manna ash, *Fraxinus ornus*.

27 One of the most famous preachers was Bernardino Ochino (1487–1564), a former Franciscan monk from Siena, a town that was considered to have the purest pronunciation of Italian.

28 Malcolm Thick, *Sir Hugh Plat. The Search for Useful Knowledge in Early Modern London.* Prospect Books, Totnes, 2010, especially pp. 119–26.

29 *Epulario, or The Italian Banquet Wherein Is Shewed the Maner How to Dresse and Prepare All Kind of Flesh, Foules or Fishes. As Also How to Make Sauces, Tartes, Pies, &c. After the Maner of All Countries. With an Addition of Many Other Profitable and Necessary Things*, A[dam] I[slip], London, 1598. It was first printed in its original language as early as 1516 in Venice and enjoyed numerous Italian editions up to 1700.

30 Thomas Palmer, *An Essay of the Meanes how to Make our Trauailes, into Forraine Countries, the More Profitable and Honourable*, H[umphrey] L[ownes], London, 1606, pp. 42–7.

31 Joan Thirsk, *Food in Early Modern England*, Continuum, London 2007, p. 212.

32 G.[ervase] M.[arkham], *The English Hus-Wife containing the inward and outward Vertues which ought to be in a complete Woman. As her skill in Physicke, Surgery, Cookery…* Nicholas Okes for Iohn Harison, London, 1631, pp. 126 and 130.

33 Fynes Moryson, *An Itinerary Containing His Ten Yeeres Travell Through the Twelve Dominions of Germany, Bohmerland, Sweitzerland, Netherland, Denmarke, Poland, Italy, Turky, France, England, Scotland & Ireland*, James MacLehose, Glasgow, 1907–8, 4 vols. Italy is dealt with mainly in vol. 1, pp. 145–384, covering the years 1593–5, and vol. 4, pp. 74–103.

34 The only beans available in Europe at the time were the black-eyed bean and the broad bean, unless some specimen of American beans had made their way to Northern Italy by the 1590s.

35 Moryson, *An Itinerary*, v. 4, p. 93.

36 This was confirmed by a later traveller, Sir Philip Skippon: 'The Italians … eat much garlic

which they put in most of their sauces', in Donatella Livia Sparti, 'Il diario di viaggio (1663–66) di Sir Philip Skippon: arte e società nell'Italia del Seicento', *Bollettino del C.I.R.V.I.*, anno XIX, vol. 37/38, fascs I/II, 1998, pp. 103–200.

37 Malcolm Thick, *The Neat House Gardens*, Prospect Books, Totnes, 1998, pp. 19–23, mentions Richard Gardiner's *Profitable instructions for the manuring, sowing and planting of kitchen gardens. Very profitable for the common wealth and greatly for the helpe and comfort of poore people*, 1599, and other relevant works dealing with 'root vegetables'.

38 Moryson, *An Itinerary*, vol. 4, p. 96. *Pasta reale* is a kind of sweet pastry made with eggs and sugar. *Ciambolini* could be a mistake for *ciambellini*, sweet biscuits with a large hole in the middle. *Gentilezze*, literally 'kindnesses', is probably the equivalent of 'subtleties' a word used by Torkington and earlier writers in some fifteenth-century recipes. This culinary subtlety is defined in the *OED* as 'An ornamental figure, scene, or other design, typically made of sugar, used as a table decoration or eaten between the courses of a meal. *hist.* after 16th cent.'

39 Moryson, *An Itinerary*, v. 4, p. 97.

40 Allen J. Grieco, 'Les plantes, les régimes végétariens et la mélancolie à la fin du Moyen Age et au début de la Renaissance italienne,' in A. J. Grieco, Odile Redon, Lucia Tongiorgi Tomasi (eds), *Le Monde végétal (XIIe–XVIIe siècles). Savoirs et usages sociaux*, Presses Universitaires de Vincennes, Saint Denis, 1993, pp. 11–29.

41 Ibid., p. 149. The birds were quite expensive, since the average daily wage for a skilled worker in Venice was twenty-four *sols*. See Robert C. Davis, *Shipbuilders of the Venetian Arsenal. Workers and Workplace in the Preindustrial City*, Johns Hopkins University Press, Baltimore and London, 1991, pp. 29–30 and pp. 102–4.

42 Pantaleone da Confienza, *Trattato dei latticini*, ed. Emilio Faccioli, Slow Food Editore, Bra, 2001, p. 78. Pantaleone da Confienza published his *Summa lacticiniorum*, a compendium on dairy products, in 1477.

43 Parmesan was known from the fourteenth century. Pope Julius II (1443–1513) offered one hundred 'wheels of Parmesan' and some barrels of wine to Henry VIII. See Catherine Fletcher, *Diplomacy in Renaissance Rome. The Rise of the Resident Ambassador*, Cambridge University Press, Cambridge, 2015, p. 150.

44 Moryson, *An Itinerary*, vol. 1, p. 201. What Moryson calls *bolinei* are probably *bolognini*, roughly equivalent to *soldi* in Venice. He paid four *bolinei* for a chamber, and five for a pound of eel.

45 The full title is *Coryats Crudities; Hastily Gobled vp in Five Moneths Trauells in France, Sauoy, Italy, Rhetia co[m]monly Called the Grisons Country, Heluetia Aliàs Switzerland, Some Parts of High Germany, and the Netherlands; Newly Digested in the Hungry Aire of Odcombe in the County of Somerset, & Now Dispersed to the Nourishment of the Trauelling Members of this Kingdome*, W[illiam] S[tansby], [London], [1611]. For the meaning of the term 'crudities' one can refer to Thomas Elyot's *The Castel of Helth*, Thomas Berthlet, London, 1539, fol. 76v, which explains it as 'a vicious concoction of things' not properly digested and therefore bringing about an imbalance in the digestive system.

46 Italian Benvenuto, *The Passenger*, T[homas] S[nodham], London, 1612, pp. 90–198.

47 See the contemporary account of Paul II's death, written by Nicodemo Tranchedini da Pontremoli, an envoy of the duke of Milan in Bruno Laurioux, *Gastronomie, humanisme et société à Rome*, pp. 341–2.

48 Ken Albala, *The Banquet: Dining in the Great Courts of Late Renaissance Europe*, University of Illinois Press, Urbana, ILL, 2007, pp. 90–104.

49 Lassels is a mine of detailed information on Italian culinary habits. He noted, for instance, that Italian hosts never presented guests with salt, 'nor serve brains of any fowls', because they did

not want to be misinterpreted of accusing the guest of being brainless or lacking wit. Richard Lassels, *The Voyage of Italy, or a Compleat Journey Through Italy*, John Starkey, Paris, 1670, p. 16.

50 Frances A. Yates, *John Florio. The Life of an Italian in Shakespeare's England*, Cambridge University Press, Cambridge, 1934.

51 Although the *OED* dates the first appearance of the word to 1760, in an unclear context, and then in 1839, Florio's '*rafiuolo*' provides an accurate description of ravioli: 'a kind of dainty paste meat made in Italy in form [of] little pies or chewets'. John Florio, *A World of Words*, Hatfield, London, 1598.

52 Florio, *A World of Words*, p. 385.

53 Bartolomeo Scappi, *Opera of Bartolomeo Scappi*, p. 492: 'To prepare flaky pizza, popularly called a dry napoleon'.

54 [Andrea Trevisan], *A Relation or Rather a True Account of the Island of England; with Sundry Particulars of the Customs of these People, and of the Royal Revenues Under King Henry the Seventh, About the Year 1500*, ed. Charlotte Augusta Sneyd, Camden Society, London, 1847, pp. 20–21.

55 'Panáce: an hearbe with a long stalke yeelding a precious baulmie liquor. Some take it for All-heale, or wound-wort, some for Tobacco, some for Cost-marie, some for Angelica, and some for Scab-wort, or Horse-heele'. Florio, *A World of Words*, p. 353.

56 Ibid., p. 616.

57 The English version bears the title *The Fruit, Herbs & Vegetables of Italy. An Offering to Lucy, Countess of Bedford*, ed. Gillian Riley, Viking and British Museum, Natural History, London, 1989. See also Barbara K. Lewalski, 'Lucy, Countess of Bedford: Images of a Jacobean Courtier and Patroness', in *Politics of Discourse. The Literature and History of Seventeenth-Century England*, Kevin Sharpe and Steve N. Zwicker (eds), University of California Press, Berkeley and London, 1987, pp. 52–77.

58 By this time, the caprificatory wasp must have reached the British isles!

59 Cardoons were later mentioned in a 1708 book by John Mortimer, *The Whole Art of Husbandry or, the Way of Managing and Improving of Land*. The Spanish painter Juan Sánchez Cotán (1560–1627), gave a vivid illustration of this vegetable in various paintings, including 'Still life with Game Fowl, Vegetables and Fruit' (now in the Prado Museum, Madrid). According to some, the cardoon may have been a symbol of the scourge used in the flagellation of Christ, just as cloves and carrots were used to symbolize the nails of the cross. See Gillian Riley, 'Parsnips: Now You See Them – Now You Don't', in *Disappearing Foods: Studies in Foods and Dishes at Risk, Proceedings of the Oxford Symposium on Food and Cookery 1994*, ed. Harlan Walker, Prospect, Totnes, 1995, pp. 154–8.

60 According to a 1728 short treatise, the best cardoon seeds came from Italy. See Malcolm Thick, 'The Contrasting Histories of Florence Fennel, Spanish Cardoons, Broccoli and Celeriac in England from the Early Eighteenth Century Until the 1970s', in *Disappearing Foods*, pp. 204–14.

61 The name given by Castelvetro, *súgoli*, comes from his Modenese dialect. It was a popular, cheap treat in Emilia Romagna, and the storyteller Giulio Cesare Croce (1550–1609) penned poems in its praise.

3. ADVENTURES IN THE SEVENTEENTH CENTURY AND BEYOND

1   In 1661 Evelyn published *Fumifugium*, a short book on the quality of London air, defined by the author a 'hellish and dismal cloud of sea-coal'. He was very much in favour of planting trees along city streets to improve the quality of the air and offset pollution. Maggie Campbell-Culver, *A Passion for Trees. The Legacy of John Evelyn*, Eden Project Books, London, 2006.

2   *The Diary of John Evelyn* (ed. Esmond Samuel De Beer, Everyman's Library, London, 2006) extends to almost 1,000 pages. His other works include an unfinished encyclopaedic work on gardening, the *Elysium Britannicum*, a project which occupied Evelyn on and off throughout his life; *Sculptura: or the History and Art of Chalcography, and Engraving in Copper* (1661); *Sylva, or a Discourse of Forest Trees*; *Pomona, or an Appendix Concerning Fruit-Trees in Relation to Cider*; and *Kalendarium Hortense*, a garden almanac; the last three titles were all printed in 1664. He also published numerous translations from Latin and French treatises, including *The French Gardiner* (1658), a translation of Nicolas de Bonnefons' *Le jardinier françois*.

3   In his diary, Evelyn condemns horse baiting with dogs as 'this wicked and barbarous sport'; and when he had to accompany some friends to a 'bear garden' where there were dog fights and bull baiting, he described those activities as 'butcherly sports, or rather barbarous cruelties'. Evelyn, *The Diary*, pp. 465 and 486.

4   Evelyn was influenced by the works of Thomas Tryon, whose *The Way to Health, Long Life and Happiness* (1683), inspired many people, including Benjamin Franklin, to become a vegetarian. As a term, vegetarianism belongs to the nineteenth century, but it was also known as the Pythagorean diet. It all started with a long speech that the Roman poet Ovid attributed to Pythagoras in his *Metamorphoses*, in which the ancient Greek scholar and mathematician accused the meat-eaters of resembling graves. (Ovid, *Metamorphoses*, bk XV, pp. 523–37.) Later supporters of vegetarianism believed that Pythagoras had travelled to India, where he had met the Brahmins, wise men and religious leaders, who lived to a ripe old age without ever eating anything of animal origin. See Tristram Stuart, *The Bloodless Revolution. A Cultural History of Vegetarianism from 1600 to Modern Times*, W.W. Norton & Company, New York and London, 2008.

5   Evelyn, *The Diary*, p. 13.

6   First printed in London by B. Tooke in 1699, the author was mentioned only as 'J. E. S. R. S. [Member of the Royal Society], Author of the *Kalendarium*'.

7   John Evelyn, *Acetaria*, ed. Christopher Driver, Prospect Books, Totnes, 1996, p. 16.

8   Ibid., p. 16.

9   Ibid., p. 54.

10 Ibid., p. 26.

11 Ibid., p. 26. Evelyn seems to have been particularly sensitive to smells, and when he reaches Bologna in May 1645, he comments in his *Diary* (p. 193): 'This City is famous also for *salsicci* [sausages], & sells a world of Parmegiano cheese, with botargo, caviar &c. which makes some of their shops perfume the streets with no agreeable smell.' See also *Taste & Smell in the Eighteenth Century*, special issue of *De Achttiende Eeuw*, v. 48, no. 1/2, 2016.

12 Among them, Evelyn may have known the work of Giovanni Battista Vigilio, who wrote a book dedicated to salads in a Mantuan chronicle of the late sixteenth century, in which he mentions a tasty concoction made up with fifteen edible plants, seven flowers, nine fruits and twelve seasonings. Giovanni Battista Vigilio, *La insalata. Cronaca mantovana dal 1561 al*

1602, Daniela Ferrari and Cesare Mozzarelli (eds), Mantua, Arcari, 1992. Another early Italian treatise on salads was penned by Salvatore Massonio, *Archidipno, ouero dell'insalata, e dell'vso di essa*, Marc'Antonio Brogiollo, Venice, 1627.

13 Evelyn, *Acetaria*, p. 18.

14 Ibid., p. 18.

15 For one of the most entertaining 'discoveries' of globe artichokes, I heartily recommend a piece by Anthony Lane: 'Choke', *The New Yorker*, v. 83, 3 September 2007, pp. 104–5.

16 Evelyn, *Acetaria*, p. 45. See also Alan Davidson, *The Oxford Companion to Food*, Oxford University Press, Oxford, 1999, p. 418.

17 Evelyn, *Acetaria*, p. 21. Swinton quoted in Jeremy Black, *Italy and the Grand Tour*, Yale University Press, New Haven and London, 2003, p. 78.

18 Evelyn, *Acetaria*, p. 25.

19 Oxford, Bodleian Library, MS. Don. e. 11, fol. 158r. Malcolm Thick, 'The Contrasting Histories of Florence Fennel…', also mentions some eighteenth-century recipes.

20 David Gentilcore, *Pomodoro! A History of the Tomato in Italy*, Columbia University Press, New York, NY, 2010.

21 Philip Miller, *The Gardeners Dictionary Containing the Methods of Cultivating and Improving the Kitchen, Fruit, Flower Garden*, [Printed for the Author], London. It ran to eight editions between 1731 and 1768.

22 Pepys went to the bear garden in London on 14 August 1666 to see some 'bull's tossing of the dogs'. *The Diary of Samuel Pepys*, ed. Henry B. Wheatley, Random House, New York, [n.d.], 2 vols, vol. II, p. 269. On the other hand, bear-baiting, bull-baiting and cock-fights were described as 'extremely pleasant' activities, by Lorenzo Magalotti, an Italian author and diplomat: *Lorenzo Magalotti at the Court of Charles II: His Relazione d'Inghilterra of 1668*, ed. William Edgar Knowles Middleton, Wilfried Laurier University Press, Waterloo, ONT, 1980, p. 127.

23 Pepys, *The Diary*, vol. II, p. 96.

24 Some recipes have been collected by Christopher Driver and Michelle Berriedale-Johnson in *Pepys at Table. Seventeenth Century Recipes for the Modern Cook*, Book Club Associates, London, 1984. See also John Fletcher, 'The Significance of Samuel Pepys's Predilection for Venison Pasty', in *Wild Food. Proceedings of the Oxford Symposium on Food and Cookery 2004*, Prospect Books, Totnes, 2006, pp. 122–30.

25 Pepys, *The Diary*, vol. II, p. 286.

26 While the value of spices remained at around £30,000 between 1622 and 1700, average London imports of wines were estimated at £274,000 between 1634 and 1640, then increased to £467,000 in 1699-1701. Sugar went from £106,000 to £526,000 over the same period, and other foodstuffs, apart from fruits and spices, rose from £52,000 to £167,000. Hard cheese is probably included in the last figures. See Gigliola Pagano De Divitiis, *English Merchants in Seventeenth-Century Italy*, Cambridge University Press, Cambridge, 1997, pp. 34–6.

27 Lassels, *The Voyage of Italy*, p. 134. This is probably an exaggeration; 200lb (about 90kg) seems a more realistic figure.

28 The poem was published in Vincent Bourne, *Poemata latine partim reddita, partim scripta*, Slatter & Munday, Oxford, 1808, p. 40.

29 Hester Lynch Piozzi, *Glimpses of Italian Society in the Eighteenth Century. From the 'Journey' of Mrs Piozzi*, Seeley & Co., London, 1892, p. 91.

30 Pepys, *The Diary*, vol. II, p. 287.

31 Robert May, *The Accomplisht Cook, or the Art and Mystery of Cookery ...*, R.W. for Nath. Brooke, London, 1660. See also Tom Jaine, 'May, Robert' in *Oxford Dictionary of National Biography* (2004).

32 *The Accomplisht Cook*, section IV, sig. 3.

33 See the entry on *brodo lardiero* in Gillian Riley, *The Oxford Companion to Italian Food*, p. 78.

34 *The Accomplisht Cook*, p. 217.

35 Ibid., p. 101. See also E. Carnevale Schianca, *La Cucina medievale*, pp. 645–6.

36 Brigid Allen, 'Foreign Flavours: The Italian Warehouse and its Near Relations in England, 1720–1880', in *Spicing up the Palate: Studies of Flavourings – Ancient and Modern. Proceedings of the Oxford Symposium on Food and Cookery 1992*, ed. Harlan Walker, Prospect, London, 1993, pp. 23–27.

37 Oxford, Bodleian Library, John Johnson Collection of Printed Ephemera, Trade Cards 12 (42) and Trade Cards 12 (45). The etching is attributed to William Hogarth.

38 William Verrall, *A Complete System of Cookery*, [Printed for the Author], London, 1759, pp. 214–15. As early as 1741 Joseph Williams in London advertises, among other groceries, *Vermajelly* on the heading of his bill, later corrected to *vermicelli*. Oxford, Bodleian Library, John Johnson Collection of Printed Ephemera, Bill Headings 12 (85).

39 Allen concludes her essay on Italian warehouses with the following comment: '"Italian", then, in the context of grocery shops, could be used to indicate the surviving traces of an oilman's business, with its concomitants of candles, pickles, scrubbing-brushes, starch and blue; or it could mean "exotic, superior, expensive and stimulating".' Allen, 'Foreign Flavours', p. 26.

40 Oxford, Bodleian Library, MS. Eng. Misc. e. 589, fol. 128b. The recipe is penned on a fragment of paper and some letters are barely legible.

41 Brigid Allen, 'Foreign Flavours', p. 25. Numerous other shops of this kind feature in the Bodleian Library's John Johnson Collection of Printed Ephemera, 'Bill Headings' 13 (54, 69, 52), and 'Bill Headings' 19 (66, 68, 69) between 1812 and 1895.

42 Ralph Rylance, *The Epicure's Almanack. Eating and Drinking in Regency London: the Original 1815 Guidebook*, ed. Janet Ing Freeman, The British Library, London, 2012. p. 134. A sample menu is also provided, p. 135, together with the relevant prices that seem very affordable. A *vermicelli* soup is 6d, and fish (boiled skate, halibut, cod and salt fish) are priced between 6d and 9d, while fried fish is 8d, as is mutton à la mode and omelette. Fowl (boiled or roasted) cost 1s 6d, macaroni 8d and potatoes 2d.

43 Oxford, Bodleian Library, John Johnson Collection of Printed Ephemera, Trade cards 9 (95) and Trade cards 11 (37a). See also Brigid Allen, 'Foreign Flavours', p. 23.

44 Brigid Allen, *Cooper's Oxford: a History of Frank Cooper Limited*, Archive Services of Oxford, Oxford, 1989.

45 They will start early in the nineteenth century in Paris. Rebecca L. Spang, *The Invention of the Restaurant. Paris and Modern Gastronomic Culture*, Harvard University Press, Cambridge, MA, 2000.

46 Giacomo Casanova, *Histoire de ma vie*, ed. Francis Lacassin, Robert Laffont, Paris, 2006, 3 vols, vol. 3, pp. 125–322. For earlier Italian views on London there are plenty of official reports of Venetian ambassadors, and the fascinating account by Lorenzo Magalotti.

47 Casanova, *Histoire de ma vie*, vol. 3, p. 127. Unfortunately he does not elaborate, but the implication is that even the air and the water 'taste' differently from France and Italy, even that of the river Thames.

48 For the possible location of the house, see Gillian Rees, 'A Residence in Pall Mall', *L'Intermédiaire des Casanovistes*, année XXIV, 2007, pp. 11–14.

49 'L'Anglais est *criofage*', he wrote, coining a word based on the Greek for 'mutton-eaters'. Casanova, *Histoire de ma vie*, vol. 3, p. 146.

50 Some English travellers to Italy, including Peter Beckford, had a different view of this dish: 'The soup is no better than broth, being the essence of the bouilli only, which, of course, is boiled to rags.' Peter Beckford, *Familiar Letters from Italy to a Friend in England*, Salisbury, 1805, 2 vols., vol. 1, p. 246.

51 Casanova, *Histoire de ma vie*, vol. 3, p. 146. As we have seen, Italian wines could be purchased in London from Italian warehouses.

52 Ibid., p. 212.

53 Ibid., p. 281.

54 Figpeckers (*beccafichi* in Italian) are small songbirds, garden warblers, who were said to fatten in the autumn when they ate figs and were considered a great delicacy.

55 Mariana Starke, *Letters from Italy*, Thomas Gillet for R. Phillips, London, 1800. See also Kathryn Walchester, *'Our own Fair Italy': Nineteenth-Century Women's Travel Writing and Italy 1800–1844*, Peter Lang, Oxford, Bern and New York, 2007, pp. 71–91.

56 Chloe Chard, *Pleasure and Guilt on the Grand Tour: Travel Writing and Imaginative Geography 1600–1830*, Manchester University Press, Manchester and New York, 1999, p. 245.

57 *Correspondence between Frances, Countess of Hertford … and Henrietta Louisa Countess of Pomfret Between the Years 1738 and 1741*, London, 1805, 3 vols, vol. III, pp. 154–246.

58 Ibid., vol. III, p. 196.

59 Black, *Italy and the Grand Tour*, p. 76.

60 Smollet declared that 'when eatables were found, we were almost poisoned by their cookery'. Tobias Smollett, *Travels Through France and Italy*, Tauris Parke Paperbacks, London, 2010, p. 285.

61 [Anna Riggs Miller], *Letters from Italy, Describing the Manners, Customs, Antiquities, Paintings, &c. of that Country, in the Years MDCCLXX and MDCCLXXI, to a Friend Residing in France by an English Woman*, Edward and Charles Dilly, London, 3 vols, 1776. Miller [*née* Riggs], Anna, Lady Miller (1741–1781), *Oxford DNB*, online edn (Elizabeth Lee, *rev.* Rebecca Mills) [http://ezproxy-prd. bodleian.ox.ac.uk:2167/view/article/18720, accessed 26 Nov 2017].

62 Black, *Italy and the Grand Tour*, p. 77.

63 *Mrs Beeton's Book of Household Management*, ed. Nicola Humble, Oxford University Press, Oxford, 2008, p. 140. Isabella Beeton's iconic book was first published in monthly supplements in *The Englishwoman's Domestic Magazine*, 1859–61.

64 Henry Sass, *A Journey to Rome and Naples, Performed in 1817; Giving an Account of the Present State of Society in Italy; and Containing Observations on the Fine Arts*, Longman, Hurst, Rees, Orme & Brown, London, 1818, pp. 4–5.

65 Aimée George, *Culinary Experiences of the Grand Tour: British Tourists on Italian Gastronomy, 1765–1900*, M.St. thesis, University of Oxford, 2008, p. 25.

66 Black, *Italy and the Grand Tour*, p. [1].

67 The *OED* records instances of *polenta* in 1398 and in the second half of the sixteenth century. Smollett also mentioned it as a 'very nourishing and agreeable' food. Tobias Smollett, *Travels through France and Italy*, p. 190.

68 Anna Del Conte, *The Classic Food of Northern Italy*, Pavilion, London 1999, p. 214.

69 Black, *Italy and the Grand Tour*, p. 78. The mould of meat pudding was probably *polpettone*, known at the time as *piccatiglio*. For a modern version, see Elizabeth David, *Italian Food*, Penguin Books, London, 1989, pp. 185–6.

70 Piozzi, *Glimpses of Italian Society*, pp. 151–2. The combination of cured ham with melon or

figs harks back to the principles of Galenic medicine, in which something like salty ham was considered 'hot and dry', and therefore had to be balanced with something 'cool and moist'.

71 *Ibid.*, p. 255.

72 Contrary to most other travellers, she found 'fat Bologna' rather sad 'from the numberless priests, friars, and women all dressed in black, who fill the streets, and stop on a sudden to pray.' *Ibid*, pp. 143-144. Mrs Piozzi was there on the day before Corpus Domini and maybe that explains the extra piety. But the following day, she was at least able to appreciate the colourful procession with candles.

73 Hester Lynch Piozzi, *Observations and Reflections Made in the Course of a Journey through France, Italy and Germany*, A. Strahan and T. Cadell, London, 1789, 2 vols, vol. 1, p. 328.

74 Michael J. Franklin, Piozzi [*née* Salusbury; *other married name* Thrale], Hester Lynch (1741-1821) *Oxford DNB* [http://ezproxy-prd.bodleian.ox.ac.uk:2167/view/10.1093/ref:odnb/9780198614128.001.0001/odnb-9780198614128-e-22309?rskey=aaonJ7&result=1, accessed 06 Dec. 2017].

75 William H. Scheuerle, 'Gardiner, Marguerite, countess of Blessington (1789-1849)', *Oxford DNB*, [http://ezproxy-prd.bodleian.ox.ac.uk:2167/view/article/2640, accessed 26 Nov 2017].

76 Her contacts with the most famous English expat of the time gave her the opportunity to publish her conversations with Byron after his death in 1824. Marguerite Blessington, *Conversations of Lord Byron*, ed. Ernest J. Lovell Jr, Princeton University Press, Princeton, NJ, 1969.

77 Her fame also reached the United States and in 1838 an American publisher in Philadelphia published *The Works of Lady Blessington* in two volumes.

78 Marguerite Blessington, *The Idler in Italy*, Henry Colburn, London, 1840, 3 vols, vol. 3, p. 245.

79 Ibid, vol. 3, pp. 259-60. Lointier was a restaurant in rue de Richelieu where men and ladies of fashion and the 'idle' congregated. See Prosper Enfantin, 'The Idle and the Workers', in *Political Economy and Industrialism: Banks in Saint-Simonian Economic Thought*, ed. Gilles Jacoud, Routledge, London, 2010, pp. 76-81.

80 James Boswell, *Life of Johnson*, George Birkbeck Norman Hill and Lawrence Fitzroy Powell (eds), Oxford University Press, Oxford, 2014, p. 285. The conversation bears the date 1778.

81 The book was written on subscription, and it became known with the title of *First Catch Your Hare* through popular humour. Jennifer Stead, 'Quizzing Glasse: or Hannah Scrutinized', in Hannah Glasse, '*First Catch Your Hare…*' *The Art of Cookery Made Plain and Easy by a Lady. A Facsimile of the First Edition*, Prospect Books, London, 2012, pp. vi-vii, xv-xxxi.

82 Hannah Glasse, *Preface to The Art of Cookery*, p. [2]: 'I have heard of a cook that used six pounds of butter to fry twelve eggs; when everybody knows, that understands cooking, that half a pound is full enough, or more than need be used. But then it would not be *French*.'

83 All the 'foreign' recipes seem to derive from *The Whole Duty of a Woman*, a popular book of advice to women, published in 1737. Jennifer Stead, 'Quizzing Glasse: or Hannah Scrutinized', pp. xvi-xvii.

84 This is the definition given in the *OED* for the medieval French form of *coulis*.

85 Glasse, '*First Catch your Hare…*', p. 54.

86 Ibid., p. 68.

87 Ibid., p. 69.

88 Ibid., pp. 29-30.

89 Ibid., p. 107.

4. THEY CALL IT MACARONI

1   Franklin's autobiography was translated twice into Italian, in 1830 and in 1869. Antonio
    Pace, 'Benjamin Franklin and Italy since the Eighteenth Century' in *Proceedings of the American
    Philosophical Society*, vol. 94, no. 3, Jun. 20, 1950, pp. 242–50.

2   The earliest mention of risotto in the *OED* is dated 1821. And one of the earliest appearances
    of this dish in high-class British menus is *Rizotto* [sic] *de foies de volaille* (risotto with chicken
    livers) in a 1905 menu of the Café Parisien du Savoy Hotel in London. See Oxford, Bodleian
    Library, John Johnson Collection, 'Menus Hotels' 3 (44).

3   Recipes for *minestra di riso* (rice soup) are provided in an anonymous collection, entitled *Il cuoco
    piemontese perfezionato a Parigi*, ed. Silvano Serventi, Slow Food Editore, Bra, 1995, pp. 70–71,
    and Vincenzo Corrado, *Il cuoco galante*, Grimaldi & C., Naples, 2013, pp. 8–9, respectively first
    published in 1766 and 1793.

4   James M. Gabler, *Passions. The Wines and Travels of Thomas Jefferson*, Bacchus Press, Baltimore,
    1995, p. 98.

5   Ibid., pp. 3–8.

6   Margherita Marchione, *The Adventurous Life of Philip Mazzei / La vita avventurosa di Filippo
    Mazzei*, University Press of America, Lonham, New York and London, 1995, pp. 58–60.

7   Ibid., p. 150.

8   James M. Gabler, *Passions*, pp. 59–79.

9   Ibid, p. 199.

10 Mary Randolph, *The Virginia Housewife, or Methodical Cook*, facsimile edition, Dover
    Publications, New York, 1993, p. 84.

11 According to the greatest Italian cookery writer of the late nineteenth century, Pellegrino
    Artusi, pure pork fat 'with a hint of bay leaf' was used for this dish in the area near Bologna.
    Pellegrino Artusi, *Science in the Kitchen and the Art of Eating Well*, translated by Murtha Baca
    and Stephen Sartarelli, University of Toronto Press, Toronto, Buffalo, and London, 2003,
    p. 173. First published in 1891, the book went through very numerous editions, and was
    extremely influential. Artusi's recipe is entitled 'Pollo fritto con pomodori' (Fried chicken
    with tomatoes), although, according to a Florentine friend, the addition of tomatoes does not
    appear in modern Tuscan practice.

12 James Fenimore Cooper, *Excursions in Italy*, pp. 32–3.

13 On the concept of 'authentic' see Joan P. Alcock, 'The Ambiguity of Authenticity' in
    Authenticity in the Kitchen. Proceedings of the Oxford Symposium on Food and Cookery 2005, ed.
    Richard Hosking, Prospect books, Totnes, 2006, pp. 33–44.

14 James Fenimore Cooper, *Excursions in Italy*, Richard Bentley, London, 1838, p. 33.

15 Ibid., p. 147.

16 Ibid., p. 252.

17 Nathaniel Hawthorne, *The French and Italian Notebooks*, ed. Thomas Woodson, Ohio State
    University Press, Columbus, OH, 1980, p. 241.

18 Ibid., pp. 290–91.

19 It is mentioned in Vincenzo Corrado's *Il cuoco galante*, p. 162.

20 Hawthorne, *The French and Italian Notebooks*, p. 291.

21 Oxford, Bodleian Library, John Johnson collection of ephemera, 'Oxford Trade' 5 and Folder
    of Trade [to be catalogued].

22 Recipes for elderflower fritters are found in early fifteenth-century Italian books. I have

myself prepared them on more than one occasion, and late May to early June is the right time for picking the flower sprays. The practice seems to have been a constant one over the centuries, and Corrado, in his *Il cuoco galante*, says: 'Elderflowers with a batter of eggs and cheese, or ricotta, make very good fritters' (p. 170).

23 Close by is 'La Foce', the Unesco World Heritage Site house and garden created by Iris Origo (1902–1988), an English writer who married an Italian aristocrat.

24 Hawthorne, *The French and Italian Notebooks*, p. 467. It may be worth noting that the normal word for 'omelette' in Italian is *frittata*. Only recently has this word taken on the meaning of Spanish *tortilla* in English. How confusing!

25 Hawthorne, *The French and Italian Notebooks*, pp. 486–515.

26 Ibid., p. 515.

27 Fenimore Cooper, *Excursions in Italy*, p. 4.

28 At some popular festivals and in some specialised country restaurants you may still find them on the menu, but I have traced very few recipes for frogs' legs in contemporary recipe books. There is one in a Michelin-starred restaurant in Lombardy, where the tiny legs are served fried in a light batter with finely chopped flat-leaf parsley and a little garlic.

29 Fenimore Cooper, *Excursions in Italy*, p. 7.

30 Ibid., p. 272.

31 Nathaniel Hawthorne, *Twenty Days with Julian and Little Bunny by Papa*, with an introduction by Paul Auster, New York Review of Books, New York, NY, 2003, p. 66.

32 John F. Mariani, *How Italian Food Conquered the World*. Palgrave MacMillan, New York, NY, 2011, p. 70.

33 Leigh Hunt, *The Autobiography of Leigh Hunt with reminiscences of Friends and Contemporaries*, Smith, Elder & Co., London, 1850, pp. 158–9.

34 John Mollard, *The Art of Cookery*, Whittaker & Co., London, 1836, p. 209. The book was first published in 1801.

35 Eliza Acton, *Modern Cookery for Private Families*, Southover Press, London 1993, p. 330.

36 Corrado, *Il Cuoco galante*, pp. 120–22.

37 Giuseppe Tomasi di Lampedusa, *The Leopard*, Vintage Books, London, 2007, p. 58.

38 Charles Dickens, *The Uncommercial Traveller*, ed. Daniel Tyler, Oxford University Press, Oxford, 2015, pp. 53–4.

39 The Italian verb *pestare* means to crush, and *pesto* was used for something crushed (e.g. in a mortar) in the fourteenth century, but with the specific meaning of 'basil sauce' it is recorded in Italian dictionaries only from 1918.

40 Charles Dickens, *American Notes, Pictures from Italy and a Child's History of England*, Chapman and Hall, London, 1895, pp. 229–30.

41 Ibid., p. 248.

42 Salvatore Battaglia (ed.), *Grande Dizionario della Lingua Italiana*, U.T.E.T., Turin, 21 vols, vol. XX, 2000, p. 751.

43 Dickens, *American Notes, Pictures from Italy*, pp. 284–5.

44 Ibid., p. 285.

5. ITALIAN FOOD IN LONDON

1 The *London Gazette* of 20 September 1688 reported ice-cream being served at a royal banquet in Stockholm, although some kind of ice-cream is documented as being available at the French court of Marie de' Medici in the first half of the seventeenth century. Caroline Liddell and Robin Weir, *Ices. The Definitive Guide*, Grub Street, London, 1993, p.12.

2 Lucio Sponza, 'Italian "Penny Ice-Men" in Victorian London', in *Food in the Migrant Experience*, ed. Anne J. Kershen, Ashgate, Aldershot, 2002, pp. 17–41. See also Lucio Sponza, *Italian Immigrants in Nineteenth-Century Britain: Realities and Images*, Leicester University Press, Leicester, 1988, pp. 94–114; Panykos Panayi, 'The Immigrant Impact Upon London Food since c.1850', in *Food and the City in Europe since 1800*, Peter J. Atkins, Peter Lummel and Derek J. Oddy (eds), Ashgate, Aldershot, 2007, pp. 189–99.

3 Henry Mayhew, *London Labour and the London Poor*, Dover Publications, New York, 1968, 4 vols, vol. 1, p. 207.

4 Paul Merton, the stand-up comedian, joked that his mother told him they played a tune when they had run out of ice-creams!

5 Italy became a unified country in 1861. Before that it consisted of the kingdom of Piedmont and Sardinia, Lombardy and Venetia, the Duchy of Parma and Piacenza, the Grand Duchy of Tuscany, the Papal States, and the Kingdom of Naples (also known as Kingdom of the Two Sicilies).

6 Tudor Allen, *Little Italy. The Story of London's Italian Quarter*, Camden Local Studies and Archives Centre, London, 2008.

7 Edwina Ehrman, Hazel Forsyth, Lucy Peltz, Cathy Ross, *London Eats Out. 500 Years of Capital Dining*, Philip Wilson, London (Museum of London), 1999, p. 84: 'Street Food' [in the 19th century], amply illustrated. Little Italy is generally recognized as a small triangle abutting Clerkenwell Road in EC1.

8 Elizabeth David, *Harvest of the Cold Months. The Social History of Ice and Ices*, Michael Joseph, London, 1994, pp. 347–9.

9 One of Gatti's warehouses has survived and it now hosts the London Canal Museum. A café-restaurant in Holborn Hill recording the partnership of Carlo Gatti and Battista Bolla in 1849 can still be seen in a late nineteenth-century painting by T.G. Fraser (reproduced on p. 78 of *London Eats Out*).

10 Recipe based on *Gunter's Modern Confectionery* (1881), quoted in Stevens-Cox, *Ice-Creams of Victoria's Reign*, pp. 6–7, but similar instructions were given in the 1820s by Guglielmo A. Jarrin, *The Italian Confectioner; or Complete Economy of Desserts: Containing the Elements of the Art, According to the Most Modern and Approved Practice*, William H. Ainsworth, London, 1827 (3rd edition), recipe 286.

11 George Dodd, *The Food of London*, Longman, London, 1856, pp. 514–21.

12 *London Eats Out*, p. 77.

13 Oxford, Bodleian Library, John Johnson Collection of Printed Ephemera, 'Bill Headings' 12 (9), and 'Bill Headings' (Scotland) [to be catalogued].

14 John Johnson Collection, 'Menus Hotels' 5 (47).

15 George Dodd, *The Food of London*, p. 511.

16 William Blanchard Jerrolds, *The Epicure's Year Book and Table Companion*, Bradbury, Evans & Co., London, 1868, pp. 30, 113.

17 Eliza Acton, *Modern Cookery for Private Families*, p. 330.

18 In 1827 the Buitoni family started commercial production of macaroni in San Sepolcro, in central Italy. In 1842 their factory produced 3,600lb of pasta per day, and a new factory opened in 1856 in Tuscany. For an outline of the success of this produce see Serventi and Sabban, *Pasta. The Story of a Universal Food*, and Franco La Cecla, *Pasta and Pizza*, Prickly Paradigm Press, Chicago, 2007.

19 Eliza Acton, *Modern Cookery for Private Families*, pp. 507–8.

20 Antonio Latini, *Lo scalco alla moderna*, Domenico Antonio Parrino e Michele Mutii, Naples, 1692. Tommaso Astarita, *The Italian Baroque Table. Cooking and Entertaining from the Golden Age of Naples*, Arizona Center for Medieval and Renaissance Studies, Tempe, Arizona, 2014. David Gentilcore, *Pomodoro! A History of the Tomato in Italy*, pp. 52–60.

21 Gentilcore, *Pomodoro!*, p. 68.

22 Charles Elmé Francatelli, *The Modern Cook. A Practical Guide to the Culinary Art in All its Branches. Adapted as well for the largest establishments, as for the use of Private Families*, Richard Bentley, Publisher in Ordinary to Her Majesty, London, 1846.

23 See Abraham Hayward, *The Art of Dining, or Gastronomy and Gastronomers*, John Murray, London, 1852, pp. 69–78. Although French chefs are exhalted, Italian products and the importance of regional cuisine are duly appreciated, especially the 'famous *minestra del riso* at Milan' (I suppose this refers to risotto), the white truffles of Piedmont, the wild boar of Rome, the *pesce reale* (royal fish) of Naples, a fillet of beef Neapolitan style, and a *timbale de macaroni*. Among the young chefs 'rising into reputation' we find a couple of Italian names: Amato and Filippo Betti.

24 Alexis Soyer, *The Modern Housewife or Ménagère. Comprising nearly one thousand receipts …*, Simkin Marshall & Co., London, 1849.

25 *Mrs Beeton's Book of Household Management*, p. 100.

26 Alexandre Dumas, *Le Comte de Monte-Cristo*, Gallimard, Paris, 1998, 2 vols, vol. 1, p. 427. Dumas's work was published in English in 1845–6.

27 Kathryn Hughes, *The Short Life and Long Times of Mrs Beeton*, Harper Perennial, London, New York, NY, 2006, especially p. 201 where the 'wholesale pilfering from Alexis Benoît Soyer' is mentioned, and pp. 396–8.

28 Charles Ranhofer's book, *The Epicurean*, was published in 1894 or 1898, see Mariani, *How Italian Food Conquered the World*, p. 20.

29 Kate Colquhoun, *Taste. The Story of Britain Through its Cooking*, Bloomsbury, London, 2007, pp. 249–50. See also E. David, *Harvest of the Cold Months*, pp. 322–5.

30 Jarrin, *The Italian Confectioner*, recipes 388 and 389.

31 Maria Gironci (ed.), *Recipes of Italian Cookery*, Gaskill, Jones & Co., London, [no date, but Bodleian Library stamp of entry 1892].

32 Lucio Sponza, *Italian Immigrants in Nineteenth-Century Britain: Realities and Images*, pp. 32–3.

33 Stephen Montagu Williams (1835–1892) was a teacher, barrister, magistrate and a philanthropist, as well as an interesting, lively writer. He left two volumes of autobiographical writings, but nothing, as far as we know, on the subject of cookery (see entry in *DNB*).

34 Gironci, *Recipes of Italian Cookery*, p. 56. The chapter dedicated to macaroni opens with detailed instructions on how to make home-made pasta with flour and one egg to every quarter pound of flour and some warm water. She says the dough should be stretched with a rolling pin then cut into strips.

35 Lt. Col. [Nathaniel] Newnham-Davis, *Dinners & Diners*, Grant Richards, London, 1901 (first ed. 1899), pp. xxi–xxiv. The list of Italian restaurants includes: Comedy, Panton Street, where a standard meal cost 2s.6d., De [Da?] Cipresso, Greek Street; Frascati's, Oxford Street; Gatti's

and Gatti and Rodesano, The Strand; Gedda's, Arundel Street; Gianella's, Oxford Street; Monico, Shaftesbury Avenue; Odone's, Victoria Street, Oxford, Euston Road; Pagani's, Great Portland Street; Pinoli's, Wardour Street; Queen's, Sloane Square; Reggiori, Chapel Street; Tivoli, Strand; Toriani's, Brompton Road; Torino, Oxford Street; Toscano, Compton Street; Veglio, Euston Road. He missed a popular one, and the largest Italian restaurant in Soho, The Florence on Rupert Street, owned by Luigi Azario. A photograph of the restaurant staff is reproduced in Rose Shepherd, *Sherlock Holmes's London*, CICO Books, London, 2015, p. 82.

36 Newnham-Davis, *Dinners & Diners*, p. 225.

37 Ibid., pp. 13–18.

38 Nicolas Soyer, *Soyer's Standard Cookery. A Complete Guide to the Art of Cooking Dainty, Varied and Economical Dishes for the Household*, Andrew Melrose, London, 1912. Nicolas was the chef of Brooks's club, and the inventor of a special paper bag which could be used to cook certain foods in the oven, just like we use parchment paper or foil.

39 Menus from restaurants such as the Café Royal, The Carlton Restaurant and The Hotel Cecil between 1898 and 1912 confirm that macaroni *au gratin* or à l'Italienne were frequently on offer, as well as *vermicelli soups*, and at The Carlton in 1912 there is even a *Poulet Rôti aux Macaroni au Gratin* on the menu. At the Café Royal some *Salami de Bologne* appear among the hors d'oeuvres, and Gorgonzola is the most prominent Italian cheese on offer. Oxford, Bodleian Library, John Johnson Collection of Printed Ephemera, 'Menus Hotel' I (9, 16, 20b, 27b, 32a, 34).

6. PIZZERIAS AND TRATTORIAS

1 As reported by 'Bon Viveur' [Fanny and Johnnie Cradock] in *Bon Viveur's London*, Andrew Dakers, London, 1954, p. 76.

2 Giovanna Princi Baccini, 'Etimo germanico e itinerario italiano di pizza', *Archivio Glottologico Italiano*, vol. 64, 1979, pp. 42–89.

3 Mario Alinei and Ephraim Nissan, 'L'etimologia semitica dell'it. *pizza* e dei suoi corradicali est-europei, turchi e dell'area semitica levantina', *Quaderni di semantica*, XXVIII, 1, June 2007, pp. 117–36. These two apparently very different theories are not necessarily mutually exclusive, as *pizza* could well be a Semitic word that developed in Germanic areas of Italy.

4 Pellegrino Artusi, *Science in the Kitchen and the Art of Eating Well*, p. 199.

5 Antonio Mattozzi, *Inventing the Pizzeria. A History of Pizza Making in Naples*, Bloomsbury, London, New York, 2015, also mentions the contribution of women pizza makers (*pizzaiole*), pp. 33–4.

6 Alexandre Dumas, *Le corricolo*, Editions Desjonquères, Paris, 1984, p. 94.

7 Kenneth Silverman, *Lightning Man: the Accursed Life of Samuel F. B. Morse*, Alfred Knopf, New York, 2003, p. 102.

8 Quoted in Alberto Capatti and Massimo Montanari, *Italian Cuisine: a Cultural History*, Columbia University Press, New York, NY, 2003, p. 25.

9 Mariani, *How Italian Food Conquered the World*, p. 44.

10 The song was by Harry Warren (born Salvatore Antonio Guaragna) and Jack Brooks. It was launched to fame in the 1953 comedy *The Caddy*, in which Martin starred with Jerry Lewis.

11 Neapolitan dialect pronunciation for *pasta e fagioli* is *pasta e fasule*, with an adaptation to American spelling. See recipes for 'pasta with cranberry beans' (*borlotti* in Italian), and in

particular *Pasta e fagioli all'ischitana*, in Arthur Schwartz, *Naples at Table: Cooking in Campania*. Harper Collins, New York, NY, 1998, pp. 102–3.

12 A 1953 TV advertisement presented by Boiardi himself is available at www.youtube.com/watch?v=6Oq1ovULf5E. Boiardi died, aged 87, in Parma (Ohio).

13 William Zellner, 'Tom Monaghan: the Fun-Loving Prince of Pizza', in *Business Week*, 8 February 1988, p. 90, quoted in Carol Helstolsky, *Pizza. A Global History*, Reaktion Books, London, 2008, p. 88.

14 Helstosky, *Pizza. A Global History*, pp. 48–73 provides more details, see also Mariani, *How Italian Food Conquered the World* and Donna Gabaccia, *We Are What We Eat*, Harvard University Press, Cambridge, MA, 1998.

15 Detailed instructions are provided online at the site: *verace pizza napoletana recipe*, www.pizzanapoletana.org/public/pdf/disciplinare%202008%20UK.pdf

16 In *Bon Viveur* Fanny and Johnnie Cradock list numerous Italian restaurants, such as Ciccio's in Kensington where, apart from classic French dishes, one can sample '*cannelloni* and a special ice-cream known as *cassata* at a cost of only 2s. 6d.'

17 William Sitwell, *Eggs or Anarchy*, Simon & Schuster, London, 2016, the biography of Lord Woolton, the Minister of Food, provides details of rationing. See also John Burnett, *Plenty & Want. A Social History of Food in England from 1815 to the Present Day*, Routledge, London, 1989, pp. 291–5 and p. 303.

18 In stories originally published in Milan newspapers, and later collected as *La farfalla di Dinard* (Dinard's butterfly) and *Fuori di casa* (Faraway from home). Montale won the Nobel Prize for Literature in 1975.

19 Alasdair Scott Sutherland, *The Spaghetti Tree. Mario and Franco and the Trattoria Revolution*, Primavera Books, London, 2009, p. 29.

20 Bill Knott, *Con Gusto: How Italian Food Conquered Britain*, Saclà UK, 2016, pp. 47–8.

21 David, *Italian Food*, p. viii.

22 The concept is attributed to the chairman of the Savoy hotels group, Sir George Smith who formulated it in 1930 as *Dans la salle les Italiens, dans la cuisine les Français*. Scott Sutherland, *The Spaghetti Tree*, p. 29.

23 'It would be a while before English middle-class diners regarded foreign staff as individuals and fellow human beings,' wrote Scott Sutherland, *The Spaghetti Tree*, p. 29.

24 Its menu for 1967 is published in Scott Sutherland, *The Spaghetti Tree*, p. 73.

25 Mario died in 2011, aged ninety-one. www.theguardian.com/lifeandstyle/2011/aug/09/mario-cassandro-obituary. Similar obituaries were published in *The Daily Telegraph* and other dailies.

26 Franco Lagattolla, *The Recipes that Made a Million*, Orbis, London, 1978, p. 10.

27 Ibid., pp. 122–4.

28 Quoted in Scott Sutherland, *The Spaghetti Tree*, p. 84.

29 A diagram in Scott Sutherland's *The Spaghetti Tree*, between pp. 68 and 69, shows this very vividly, with an indication of the date most trattorias opened.

30 The story of this venerable institution has been told by Mary Contini, a director of Valvona & Crolla, in two books dedicated to her daughters: *Dear Francesca, An Italian Journey of Recipes Recounted with Love*, Ebury Press London, 2003, and *Dear Olivia. An Italian Journey of Love and Courage*, Canongate, Edinburgh, New York, NY, 2007, with regional recipes and detailed information on Italian products.

31 Ann and Franco Taruschio, *Leaves from the Walnut Tree: Recipes of a Lifetime*, Pavilion Books, London, 1993, pp. 9–13.

7 FROM MARKETS TO SUPERMARKETS

1   It should of course be 'panino', 'panini' being the plural form, but Anglo-Italian terms are also a testimony of the popularity of new ingredients and foods.

2   Chris Giles, 'What has the EU done for Britain?', *The Financial Times*, 31 March 2017.

3   Angela Hartnett, BBC Radio 4, *Desert Island Discs*, 14 January 2018.

4   Spaghetti, and Heinz spaghetti soup, were on sale in Sainsbury's shops as early as 1929, macaroni, spaghetti and vermicelli in 1933, but sales increased in the 1970s. I am grateful to Sainsbury's Archives for guiding me to the relevant price lists: http://catalogue.sainsburysarchive.org.uk/CalmView/Record.aspx?src=CalmView. Catalog&id=SA%2fMARK%2fADV%2f3%2f3%2f3%2f8&pos=1.

5   Patience Gray and Primrose Boyd, *Plats du jour*, Penguin, Harmondsworth, 1957. See also Patience Gray, *Honey from a Weed. Fasting and Feasting in Tuscany, Catalonia, the Cyclades and Apulia*, Prospect, London, 1986, written over a long period of time. See also Adam Federman, *Fasting and Feasting: the Life of Patience Gray, a Visionary Food Writer*, Chelsea Green, White River Junction, VT, 2017.

6   See *Plats du Jour*, pp. 100–101.

7   Marcella Hazan, *The Classic Italian Cookbook*, Macmillan, London, 1981, p. 393.

8   According to Italian law, traditional balsamic vinegar is a product certified as made according to strict rules and only in a specific area. The adjective *tradizionale* is only allowed on the mature, proper balsamic. Most varieties of commercial 'balsamic vinegar from Modena' are actually produced in various parts of Italy, or even abroad, and many customers are being duped by the label, even if some brands may be perfectly suitable for use in salads. See also Gillian Riley, 'Balsamic vinegar', in *The Oxford Companion to Italian Food*, Oxford University Press, Oxford, 2007, pp. 35–7.

9   For a flamboyant view of pasta and its effects see Patrick Leigh-Fermor, 'Gluttony', in *The Seven Deadly Sins*, Sunday Times Publications, 1962, London, pp. 256–7.

10 *The Cook Who Changed Our Lives*, BBC2, 2016, narrated by Nigella Lawson, in which Anna was defined as 'the godmother of Italian food in Britain'.

11 'The language of food', *The Financial Times*, 31 July 2010. See also M. F. K. Fisher, *The Gastronomical Me*, Daunt Books, London, 2017.

12 Alice Waters, *Chez Panisse Cookbook*, Harper Books, New York, NY, 1999, and Alice Waters, *Coming to my Senses*, Hardie Grant, London, 2017.

13 In January 2008 the *Guardian* included Petrini in a list of 50 people 'who might save the planet'. *Time* magazine recognized him as a 'European Hero' in 2004. Among the successes of the Slow Food movement was the foundation, in 2004, of an International University of Gastronomic Sciences in Pollenzo, near Turin, considered by some as a very expensive enterprise. In Bologna a large market for food and equipment concerning food production, known as FICO (*Fabbrica Italiana Contadina*, literally Italian farmers' manufacturers), was opened in 2016 by World-Eataly.

14 Numerous publications exist against animal farming, and monocultures (large-scale cultivation of only one type of cereal or legume, such as maize or soya). See Michael Pollan's *The Omnivore's Dilemma: the Search for a Perfect Meal in a Fast-food World*, Bloomsbury, London, 2006. For the Slow Food movement, see Carlo Petrini, *Slow Food, the Case for Taste*, Columbia University Press, New York, NY, 2003. Wendy Parkins and Geoffrey Craig, 'Slow Food' in Parkins and Craig, *Slow Living*, Oxford, New York, Berg, 2006, pp. 18–37; Carlo Petrini and

Gigi Padovani, *Slow Food, Storia di un'utopia possibile*, Giunti-Slow Food Editore, Florence, 2017.

15 This is explored in more detail in John Burnett, *Plenty & Want*, pp. 326–7.

16 Sophia Loren, *Eat With Me*, Michael Joseph , London, 1972. The 'digression' is on pp. 62–3. The Italian edition *In cucina con amore* (In the kitchen with love) was published in Milan by Rizzoli in 1971.

17 Sophie Loren, *Eat with me*, pp. 29–33.

18 Rose Gray and Ruth Rogers, *The River Café Cook Book*, Ebury Press, London, 1995, p. 9. See also Alexander Gilmour, 'Artful Rogers', *Financial Times Weekend*, 22 September 2017, p. 20.

19 A decade later an enterprising ex-Formula One champion, Jody Scheckter, started rearing buffaloes on his organic farm in Hampshire and producing excellent buffalo mozzarella.

20 An article in the Italian daily, *Corriere della Sera* (6 September 2010), revealed that this type of tomato, whose origin is protected by law, is actually derived from Israeli seeds.

21 Such as Clarke's, the celebrated restaurant founded by Sally Clarke in London's Kensington Church Street, which followed Alice Waters' principles.

22 Specifically, it was the TV producer Pat Llewellyn who launched Jamie Oliver's onscreen career, after great success with other TV food programmes. See obituary by Martha Kearney, *The Guardian*, 4 November 2017.

23 Jamie Oliver, *Jamie's Italy*, Michael Joseph, London, 2005, a celebration of a journey through a number of Italian regions and of their culinary traditions and favourite dishes.

24 This dessert was probably invented in a restaurant near Treviso, in the Veneto region, around 1983.

25 *Nigella Bites* (2001) and *Nigellissima* (2012), both published by Chatto & Windus, London.

26 To cite just one example, an episode of the BBC's *Inside the Factory*: 'Pasta', broadcast on 25 July 2017, revealed that some pesto produced commercially by Barilla is made with cashew nuts, instead of the more expensive pine nuts.

27 Sainsbury's Archives: http://catalogue.sainsburysarchive.org.uk/CalmView/Record. aspx?src=CalmView.Catalog&id=SA%2fMARK%2f1

28 Quoted by Annette Cozzi, *The Discourses of Food in Nineteenth-Century British Fiction*, Palgrave Macmillan, London, 2010, p. 1.

29 Burton Anderson, 'Culatello, the fugitive king of the foggy bottoms', in Burton Anderson and Scott Baldwin, *Pleasures of the Italian Table: Italy's Celebrated Foods and the Artisans Who Make Them*, Viking, London, 1994, pp. 197–221. See also G. Riley, *The Oxford Companion to Italian Food*, pp. 150–51.

30 The discovery of both *burrata* and *'nduja* is attributed to Jamie Oliver, who in an article by Mark Edmonds in the *Financial Times Magazine* (1–2 September, 2018, pp. 14–15) was defined as 'Britain's most successful chef of all time'.

31 *Poggio* is a common place name, indicating a small hill.

32 Gordon Ramsay, *Sunday Lunch and Other Recipes from the World*, London, Quadrille, 2006, pp.140–44, where he offers 'Italian essence', chicken with Marsala wine and later 'Italian sausages with lentils' and 'Parma ham, sage and Parmesan puffs'.

33 Angela Hartnett, *Cucina: Three Generations of Italian Family Cooking*, Ebury, London, 2007.

BIBLIOGRAPHY

Acton, E., *Modern Cookery for Private Families*, Southover Press, London, 1993.

Albala, K., *The Banquet: Dining in the Great Courts of Late Renaissance Europe*, University of Illinois Press, Urbana, IL, 2007.

Alberini, M., 'The Sweet and Salt Taste in Italian Renaissance Cooking', in *Taste* (Oxford Symposium on Food & Cookery 1987), ed. Tom Jaine, Prospect Books, London, 1988, pp. 15–17.

Alcock, J.P., 'The Ambiguity of Authenticity', in *Authenticity in the Kitchen* (Oxford Symposium on Food and Cookery 2005), ed. Richard Hosking, Prospect Books, Totnes, 2006, pp. 33–44.

Alcock, J.P., *Food in Roman Britain*, Tempus, Stroud, 2001.

Allen, B., *Cooper's Oxford: a History of Frank Cooper Limited*, Archive Services of Oxford, Oxford, 1989.

Allen, B., 'Foreign Flavours: The Italian Warehouse and its Near Relations in England, 1720–1880', in *Spicing up the Palate: Studies of Flavourings – Ancient and Modern* (Oxford Symposium on Food and Cookery 1992), ed. Harlan Walker, Prospect, London, 1993, pp. 23–7.

Allen, T., *Little Italy. The Story of London's Italian Quarter*, Camden Local Studies and Archives Centre, London, 2008.

Anderson, B., and Baldwin, S., *Pleasures of the Italian Table: Italy's Celebrated Foods and the Artisans Who Make Them*, Viking, London, 1994.

Apicius, *Cookery and Dining in Imperial Rome*, ed. Joseph Dommers Vehling, Dover Publications, New York, 1977.

Artusi, P., *Science in the Kitchen and the Art of Eating Well*, translated by Murtha Baca and Stephen Sartarelli, University of Toronto Press, Toronto, ONT, 2003.

Astarita, T., *The Italian Baroque Table. Cooking and Entertaining from the Golden Age of Naples*, Arizona Center for Medieval and Renaissance Studies, Tempe, AZ, 2014.

Ballerini, L. J. Parzen and S. Barzini (eds), *The Art of Cooking. The First Modern Cookery Book Composed by the Eminent Maestro Martino of Como*, University of California Press, Berkeley, CA, 2005.

Beckford, P., *Familiar Letters from Italy to a Friend in England*, 2 vols, J. Easton, Salisbury, 1805.

Beeton, I. M., *Mrs Beeton's Book of Household Management*, ed. Nicola Humble, Oxford University Press, Oxford, 2008.

Benporat, C., *Cucina italiana del Quattrocento*, Olschki, Florence, 1996.

Benvenuto, I., *The Passenger*, T[homas] S[nodham], London, 1612.

Black, J., *Italy and the Grand Tour*, Yale University Press, New Haven, CT and London, 2003.

Blanchard Jerrolds, W., *The Epicure's Year Book and Table Companion*, Bradbury, Evans & Co., London, 1868.

Blessington, M., *The Idler in Italy*, 3 vols, Henry Colburn, London, 1840.

Blessington, M., *Conversations of Lord Byron*, ed. Ernest J. Lovell Jr., Princeton University Press, Princeton, NJ, 1969.

Blumenthal, H., *Historic Heston*, Bloomsbury, London, 2013.

Boccaccio, G., *Decameron*, ed. Vittore Branca, Mondadori, Milan, 1976.

'Bon Viveur' [Fanny and Johnnie Cradock], *Bon Viveur's London*, Andrew Dakers, London, 1954.

Borde, A., *Gli itinerari d'Europa. The Introduction of Knowledge*, ed. Maria Palermo Concolato, Liguori, Naples, 1992.

Boswell, J., *Life of Johnson*, George Birkbeck Norman Hill and Lawrence Fitzroy Powell (eds), Oxford University Press, Oxford, 2014.

Bourne, V., *Poemata latine partim reddita, partim scripta*, Slatter & Munday, Oxford, 1808.

Bowman, A. K., *Life and Letters on the Roman Frontier. Vindolanda and its People*, British Museum, London, 1994.

Brears, P. *Cooking and Dining in Medieval England*, Prospect Books, Totnes, 2008.

Burnett, J., *Plenty & Want. A Social History of Food in England from 1815 to the Present Day*, Routledge, London, 1985.

Caesar, J., *The Gallic War*, ed. Henry J. Edwards, Harvard University Press, Cambridge, MA, and London, 1917.

Campbell-Culver, M., *A Passion for Trees. The Legacy of John Evelyn*, Eden Project Books, London, 2006.

Capatti, A., and Montanari, M., *Italian Cuisine: a Cultural History*, Columbia University Press, New York, NY, 2003.

Carluccio, A., *A Passion for Mushrooms*, Pavilion Books, London, 1990.

Carluccio, A., and Cataldo, G., *Two Greedy Italians*, Quadrille, London, 2011.

Carnevale Schianca, E., *La cucina medievale. Lessico, storia, preparazioni*. Olschki, Florence, 2011.

Casanova, G., *Histoire de ma vie*, 3 vols, ed. Francis Lacassin, Robert Laffont, Paris, 2006.

Castelvetro, G., *The Fruit, Herbs & Vegetables of Italy. An Offering to Lucy, Countess of Bedford*, ed. Gillian Riley, Viking and British Museum, Natural History, London, 1989.

Cato, M. P., *On Agriculture*, William Davis Hooper and Harrison Boyd (eds), Harvard University Press and Heinemann, Cambridge, MA, and London, 1979.

Chaney, E., *The Evolution of the Grand Tour. Anglo-Italian Cultural Relations Since the Renaissance*, Frank Cass, London, 1998.

Chard, C., *Pleasure and Guilt on the Grand Tour: Travel Writing and Imaginative Geography 1600–1830*, Manchester University Press, Manchester and New York, 1999.

Colgrave, B., and R. A. B. Mynors (eds), *Bede's Ecclesiastical History of the English People*, Clarendon Press, Oxford, 1969.

Colquhoun, K., *Taste. The Story of Britain Through its Cooking*, Bloomsbury, London, 2007.

Contini, M., *Dear Francesca, An Italian Journey of Recipes Recounted with Love*, Ebury Press, London, 2003.

Contini, M., *Dear Olivia. An Italian Journey of Love and Courage*, Canongate, Edinburgh and New York, NY, 2007.

Corbishley, G., *Appetite for Change: Food and Cooking in the 20th century*, English Heritage, London, 1993.

Corrado, V., *Il cuoco galante (1793)*, Grimaldi & C., Naples, 2013.

Correspondence between Frances, Countess of Hertford … and Henrietta Louisa Countess of Pomfret Between the Years 1738 and 1741, 3 vols, R. Phillips, London, 1805.

Coryat, T., *Coryats Crudities; Hastily Gobled vp in Five Moneths Trauells in France, Sauoy, Italy, Rhetia co[m]monly Called the Grisons Country, Heluetia Aliàs Switzerland, Some Parts of High Germany, and the Netherlands; Newly Digested in the Hungry Aire of Odcombe in the County of Somerset, & Now Dispersed to the Nourishment of the Trauelling Members of this Kingdome*, W[illiam S[tansby], [London], [1611].

Cozzi, A., *The Discourses of Food in Nineteenth-Century British Fiction*, Palgrave Macmillan, London, 2010.

Crystal, D., and Crystal, B., *Shakespeare's Words. A Glossary & Language Companion*, Penguin Books, London, 2002.

Cummings, C., *Food and Society in Late Roman Britain: Determining Dietary Patterns Using Stable Isotopes Analysis*, D. Phil. thesis, University of Oxford, 2008.

Curtis, R. I., *Garum and Salsamenta: Production and Commerce in Materia Medica*, Brill, Leiden, 1991.

da Confienza, P., *Trattato dei latticini*, ed. Emilio Faccioli, Slow Food Editore, Bra, 2001.

David, E., *Italian Food*, Penguin Books, London, 1989.

David, E., *Harvest of the Cold Months. The Social History of Ice and Ices*, Michael Joseph, London, 1994.

Davidson, A., *The Oxford Companion to Food*, Oxford University Press, Oxford, 1999.

Davis, R.C., *Shipbuilders of the Venetian Arsenal. Workers and Workplace in the Preindustrial City*, Johns Hopkins University Press, Baltimore, MD and London, 1991.

Del Conte, A., *Gastronomy of Italy*, Pavilion Books, London, 2013.

Del Conte, A. 'The Taste of Naples in the 18th Century', in *Taste* (Oxford Symposium on Food and Cookery 1987), ed. Tom Jaine, Prospect Books, London 1988, pp. 57–8.

Dickens, C., *American Notes, Pictures from Italy and a Child's History of England*, Chapman and Hall, London, 1895.

Dickens, C., *The Uncommercial Traveller*, ed. Daniel Tyler, Oxford University Press, Oxford, 2015.

Dickie, J., *Delizia! The Epic History of the Italians and Their Food*, Sceptre, London, 2007.

Dickson Wright, C., *A History of English Food*, Random House, London, 2011.

Dodd, G., *The Food of London*, Longman, London, 1856.

Downie, D., 'A Roman Anchovy's Tale', *Gastronomica*, 3, No 2 (Spring 2003), pp. 25–8.

Driver, C., and M. Berriedale-Johnson, *Pepys at Table. Seventeenth Century Recipes for the Modern Cook*, Book Club Associates, London, 1984.

Dumas, A., *Le corricolo. Impressions de voyage à Naples*, Editions Desjonquères, Paris, 1984.

Ehrman, E., H. Forsyth, L. Peltz and C. Ross, *London Eats Out. 500 Years of Capital Dining*, Philip Wilson, London (Museum of London), 1999.

Elyot, T., *The Castel of Helth*, Thomas Berthlet, London, 1539.

Enfantin, P., 'The Idle and the Workers', in Gilles Jacoud (ed.), *Political Economy and Industrialism: Banks in Saint-Simonian Economic Thought*, Routledge, London, 2010.

Epulario, or The Italian Banquet Wherein Is Shewed the Maner How to Dresse and Prepare All Kind of Flesh, Foules or Fishes. As Also How to Make Sauces, Tartes, Pies, &c. After the Maner of All Countries. With an Addition of Many Other Profitable and Necessary Things, A[dam] I[slip], London, 1598.

Evelyn, J., *Acetaria. A Discourse of Sallets*, ed. Christopher Driver, Prospect Books, Totnes, 1996.

Evelyn, J., *The Diary of John Evelyn*, ed. Esmond Samuel De Beer, Everyman's Library, London, 2006.

Federman, A., *Fasting and Feasting: the Life of Patience Gray, a Visionary Food Writer*, Chelsea Green, White River Junction, VT, 2017.

Fenimore Cooper, J., *Excursions in Italy*, Richard Bentley, London, 1838.

Fisher, M. F. K., *The Gastronomical Me*, Daunt Books, London, 2017.

Flandrin, J.-L., 'Les légumes dans les livres de cuisine français, du XIVe au XVIIIe siècle', in A. J. Grieco, O. Redon, L. Tangiorgi Tomasi (eds) *Le Monde végétal (XIIe–XVIIe siècles)*, Presses Universitaires de Vincennes, Saint-Denis, 1993.

Flandrin J-L., M. Montanari and A. Sonnenfeld (eds), *Food: a Culinary History from Antiquity to the Present*, Columbia University Press, New York, NY, 2013. Especially: Grieco, A. J., 'Food and Social Classes in Late Medieval and Renaissance Italy', pp. 272–82.

Fletcher, C., *Diplomacy in Renaissance Rome. The Rise of the Resident Ambassador*, Cambridge University Press, Cambridge, 2015.

Fletcher, J., 'The Significance of Samuel Pepys's Predilection for Venison Pasty', in *Wild Food* (Oxford Symposium on Food and Cookery 2004), Prospect Books, Totnes, 2006, pp. 122–30.

Florio, J., *A World of Words*, Hatfield, London, 1598.

Francatelli, C. E., *The Modern Cook. A Practical Guide to the Culinary Art in All its Branches. Adapted as well for the largest establishments, as for the use of Private Families*, Richard Bentley, Publisher in Ordinary to Her Majesty, London, 1846.

Franklin, B., *The Autobiography of Benjamin Franklin*, Airmont Publishing Company, New York, 1965.

Gabaccia, D., *We Are What We Eat*, Harvard University Press, Cambridge, MA, 1998.

Gabler, J. M., *Passions. The Wines and Travels of Thomas Jefferson*, Bacchus Press, Baltimore, MD, 1995.

Gautier, A., *Le festin dans l'Angleterre Anglo-Saxonne (Ve–XIe siècles)*, Presses Universitaires de Rennes, Rennes, 2006.

Gentilcore, D., *Pomodoro! A History of the Tomato in Italy*, Columbia University Press, New York, NY, 2010.

George, A., *Culinary Experiences of the Grand Tour: British Tourists on Italian Gastronomy, 1765–1900*, M. St. thesis, University of Oxford, 2008.

Giles, C., 'What has the EU done for Britain?', *Financial Times*, 31 March 2017.

Gilmour, A., 'Artful Rogers', *Financial Times Weekend*, 22 September 2017, p. 20.

Gironci, M. (ed.), *Recipes of Italian Cookery*, Gaskill, Jones & Co., London, [no date, but Bodleian Library stamp of entry 1892].

Goodman, A., *Margery Kempe and Her World*, Longman, Harlow, 2002.

Gray, P., and P. Boyd, *Plats du jour*, Penguin, Harmondsworth, 1957.

Gray, P., *Honey from a Weed. Fasting and Feasting in Tuscany, Catalonia, the Cyclades and Apulia*, Prospect, London, 1986.

Gray, R., and R. Rogers, *The River Café Cook Book*, Ebury Press, London, 1995; *River Café Cook Book Two*, Ebury Press, London, 1997.

Grieco, A. J., (ed.), *The Meal*, Scala Publications, London, 1992.

Grieco, A. J., 'Les plantes, les regimes végétariens et la mélancolie à la fin du Moyen Age et au début de la Renaissance italienne', in A. J. Grieco, O. Redon, L. Tangiorgi Tomasi (eds), *Le Monde végétal (XIIe–XVIIe siècles)*, Presses Universitaires de Vincennes, Saint-Denis, 1993.

Grocock, C., and S. Grainger (eds), *Apicius, a critical edition with an introduction and English Translation*, Prospect Books, London, 2006.

Guildford, R., *The Pylgrymage of Sir Richard Guylforde to the Holy Land, A.D. 1506: from a Copy Believed to Be Unique, from the Press of Richard Pynson*, ed. Henry Ellis, Camden Society, London, 1851.

Hagen, A., *Anglo-Saxon Food and Drink: Production, Processing, Distribution and Consumption*, Anglo-Saxon Books, Hockwold cum Wilton, 2006.

Hartnett, A., *Cucina: Three Generations of Italian Family Cooking*, Ebury Press, London, 2007.

Hawthorne, N., *The French and Italian Notebooks*, ed. Thomas Woodson, Ohio State University Press, Columbus, OH, 1980.

Hawthorne, N., *Twenty Days with Julian & Little Bunny by Papa*, New York Review of Books, New York, NY, 2003.

Hayward, A., *The Art of Dining, or Gastronomy and Gastronomers*, John Murray, London, 1852.

Hazan, M., *The Classic Italian Cookbook*, Macmillan, London, 1981.

Helstolsky, C., *Pizza. A Global History*, Reaktion Books, London, 2008.

Hieatt, C. B., 'Milk: Almond vs. Cow in Medieval English Courtly Cookery', in *Taste* (Oxford Symposium on Food & Cookery 1987), ed. Tom Jaine, Prospect Books, London, 1988, pp. 70–73.

Hieatt, C. B., and S. Butler (eds), *Curye on Inglysch. English Culinary Manuscripts of the Fourteenth Century (Including the Forme of Cury)*, Oxford University Press, London, 1985.

Hieatt, C. B., 'A cook of 14th-century London: Chaucer's Hogge of Ware', in *Cooks & Other People* (Oxford Symposium on Food and Cookery 1995), ed. Harlan Walker, Prospect Books, Totnes, 1996, pp. 138–43.

Hoby, T., 'The Travels and Life of Sir Thomas Hoby Kt. of Bisham Abbey, Written by Himself, 1547–1564', ed. Edgar Powell, in *The Camden Miscellany*, vol. 10, pp. v–xxiv and pp. 1–144.

Houston Bowden, G., *British Gastronomy. The Rise of Great Restaurants*, Chatto & Windus, London, 1975.

Hughes, K., *The Short Life and Long Times of Mrs Beeton*, Harper Perennial, London and New York, NY, 2006.

Hunt, L., *The Autobiography of Leigh Hunt with Reminiscences of Friends and Contemporaries*, Smith, Elder & Co., London, 1850.

Informac[i]on for pylgrymes vnto the Holy Londe, [Wynkyn de Word, London, 1500?].

Jarrin, G.A., *The Italian Confectioner; or Complete Economy of Desserts: Containing the Elements of the Art, According to the Most Modern and Approved Practice*, William H. Ainsworth, London, 1827.

Jensen Wallach, J., *How America Eats. A Social History of U.S. Food and Culture*, Rownsan & Littlefield, Lanham, MD, 2013.

Juniper, B.E., and D.J. Mabberley, *The Story of the Apple*, Timber Press, Portland, OR, 2006.

Kempe, M., *The Book of Margery Kempe. The Text from the Unique Ms. Owned by Colonel W. Butler-Bowdon*, Sanford Brown Meech and Hope Emily Allen (eds), Early English Text Society, Rochester, NY, and Woodbridge, 1997.

Knott, B., *Con Gusto: How Italian Food Conquered Britain*, Saclà UK, 2016.

La Cecla, F., *Pasta and Pizza*, Prickly Paradigm Press, Chicago, IL, 2007.

Lagattolla, F., *The Recipes that Made a Million*, Orbis, London, 1978.

Lane, A., 'Choke', *The New Yorker*, v. 83, 3 September 2007, pp. 104–105.

Lassels, R., *The Voyage of Italy, or a Compleat Journey Through Italy*, John Starkey, Paris [London], 1670.

Laurioux, B., 'Spices in the Medieval Diet. A New Approach', in *Food & Foodways: Explorations in the History and Culture of Human Nourishment*, vol. 1, no. 1, 1985, pp. 43–75.

Laurioux, B., *Le Règne de Taillevent. Livres et pratiques culinaires à la fin du Moyen Âge*, Publications de la Sorbonne, Paris, 1997.

Laurioux, B., *Gastronomie, humanisme et société à Rome au milieu du XVe siècle: autour du* De honesta voluptate *de Platina*, Edizioni Galluzzo-SISMEL, Florence, 2006.

Lawson, N., *How to Eat. The Pleasures and Principles of Good Food*, Chatto & Windus, London, 1998.

Lawson, N., *Nigella Bites*, Chatto & Windus, London, 2001.

Lawson, N., *Nigellissima. Instant Italian Inspiration*, Chatto & Windus, London 2012.

Lewalski, B. K., 'Lucy, Countess of Bedford: Images of a Jacobean Courtier and Patroness', in Kevin Sharpe and Steve N. Zwicker (eds), *Politics of Discourse. The Literature and History of Seventeenth-Century England*, University of California Press, Berkeley, CA, 1987.

Latini, A., *Lo scalco alla moderna*, Domenico Antonio Parrino e Michele Mutii, Naples, 1692.

Le Goff, J., *The Birth of Purgatory*, Scolar Press, London, 1984.

Libro della cucina del sec. XIV, Commissione per i Testi di Lingua, Bologna, 1968 [reproduction of 1863 edition].

Liddell, C., and R. Weir, *Ices. The Definitive Guide*, Grub Street, London, 1993.

Lisi, M., *Sulle tracce della Vernaccia dal XIII al XXI secolo*, Nuova Immagine, Siena, 2013.

Loren, S., *In cucina con amore*, Rizzoli, Milan, 1971. (English version: *Eat With Me*, Michael Joseph, London, 1972.)

Lyly, J., *Euphues. The Anatomy of Wit*, Gabriel Cawood, London, [1578].

Lynch Piozzi, H., *Observations and Reflections Made in the Course of a Journey through France, Italy and Germany*, 2 vols, A. Strahan and T. Cadell, London, 1789.

Lynch Piozzi, H., *Glimpses of Italian Society in the Eighteenth Century. From the 'Journey' of Mrs Piozzi*, Seeley & Co., London, 1892.

Magalotti, L., *Lorenzo Magalotti at the Court of Charles II: His Relazione d'Inghilterra of 1668*, ed. William Edgar Knowles Middleton, Wilfried Laurier University Press, Waterloo, ONT, 1980.

Marchione, M., *The Adventurous Life of Philip Mazzei/ La vita avventurosa di Filippo Mazzei*, University Press of America, Lonham, NY and London, 1995.

Mariani, J. F., *How Italian Food Conquered the World*, Palgrave MacMillan, New York, NY, 2011.

Martellotti, A., *Il 'Liber de ferculis' di Giambonino da Cremona. La gastronomia araba in Occidente nella trattatistica dietetica*, Schena, Fasano di Puglia, 2001.

Martellotti, A., *I ricettari di Federico II*, Olschki, Florence, 2005.

Mason, L., 'Alexis Jarrin: An Italian Confectioner in London', *Gastronomica*, 1, No. 2 (Spring 2001), pp. 50–64.

Massonio, S., *Archidipno, ouero dell'insalata, e dell'vso di essa*, Marc'Antonio Brogiollo, Venice, 1627.

Mayes, F., *Under the Tuscan Sun*, Bantam, London, 1998.

Mayes, F. and E., *The Tuscan Sun Cookbook: Recipes from our Italian Kitchen*, Random House, 2012.

Mayhew, H., *London Labour and the London Poor*, 4 vols, Dover Publications, New York, NY, 1968.

Mazzei, F., *Memoirs of the Life and Peregrinations of the Florentine Philip Mazzei 1730–1816*, translated by Howard R. Marraro, Columbia University Press, New York, NY, 1942.

Mead, W.E., *The English Medieval Feast*, Allen & Unwin, London, 1967.

Melville, H., *Journal of a Visit to Europe and the Levant, October 11, 1856–May 6, 1857*, Howard C. Horsford (ed.), Princeton University Press, Princeton, NJ, 1955.

Mennell, S., *All Manners of Food. Eating and Taste in England and France from the Middle Ages to the Present*, Blackwell, Oxford, 1985.

Miller, P., *The Gardeners Dictionary Containing the Methods of Cultivating and Improving the Kitchen, Fruit, Flower Garden*, [Printed for the Author], London, 1731.

Mollard, J., *The Art of Cookery*, Whittaker & Co., London, 1836.

Montanari, M., *Alimentazione e cultura nel Medioevo*, Laterza, Bari, 1988.

Montanari, M., *Il sugo della storia*, Laterza, Bari, 2016.

Mortimer, J., *The Whole Art of Husbandry; or, the Way of Managing and Improving of Land*, H. Mortlock and J. Robinson, London, 1708.

Moryson, F., *An Itinerary Containing His Ten Yeeres Travell Through the Twelve Dominions of Germany, Bohmerland, Sweitzerland, Netherland, Denmarke, Poland, Italy, Turky, France, England, Scotland & Ireland*, 4 vols, James MacLehose, Glasgow, 1907–8.

Nash, T., *The Works of Thomas Nashe*, 5 vols, Ronald Brunlees McKerrow and Frank Percy Wilson (eds), Blackwell, Oxford, 1958.

Nasrallah, N., *Delights from the Garden of Eden. A Cookbook of the Iraqi Cuisine*, Equinox, Sheffield and Bristol, 2013.

Newnham-Davis, N., *Dinners & Diners*, Grant Richards, London, 1901.

Oliver, J., *Jamie's Italy*, Michael Joseph, London, 2005.

Pace, A., 'Benjamin Franklin and Italy since the Eighteenth Century', in *Proceedings of the American Philosophical Society*, vol. 94, no. 3, Jun. 20, 1950, pp. 242–50.

Pagano De Divitiis, G., *English Merchants in Seventeenth-Century Italy*, Cambridge University Press, Cambridge, 1997.

Palmer, T., *An Essay of the Meanes how to Make our Trauailes, into Forraine Countries, the More Profitable and Honourable*, H[umphrey] L[ownes], London, 1606.

Panayi, P., 'The Immigrant Impact upon London Food since c.1850', in Peter J. Atkins, Peter Lummel and Derek J. Oddy (eds), *Food and the City in Europe since 1800*, Ashgate, Aldershot, 2007.

Parkins, W., and Craig, G., 'Slow Food' in *Slow Living*, Berg, Oxford and New York, 2006.

Pepys, S., *The Diary of Samuel Pepys*, 2 vols, ed. Henry B. Wheatley, Random House, New York, [n.d.].

Petrini, C., *Slow Food, the Case for Taste*, Columbia University Press, New York, NY, 2003.

Petrini, C., and G. Padovani, *Slow Food, Storia di un'utopia possibile*, Giunti-Slow Food Editore, Florence, 2017.

Pinnavaia, L., *The Italian Borrowings in the Oxford English Dictionary: a Lexicographical, Linguistic and Cultural Analysis*, Bulzoni, Rome, 2001.

Platina (Bartolomeo Sacchi), *On Right Pleasure and Good Health: a Critical Edition and Translation of 'De Honesta Voluptate et Valetudine'*, ed. Mary Ella Milham, Medieval & Renaissance Texts & Studies, Tempe, AZ, 1998.

Platina, *De honesta voluptate et valetudine. Un trattato sui piaceri della tavola e la buona salute*, ed. E. Carnevale Schianca, Olschki, Florence, 2015.

Pliny, *Natural History*, ed. H. Rackham, Heinemann and Harvard University Press, London and Cambridge, MA, 1945.

Pollan, M., *The Omnivore's Dilemma: the Search for a Perfect Meal in a Fast-food World*, Bloomsbury, London, 2006.

Prest, J., *The Garden of Eden. The Botanic Garden and the Re-Creation of Paradise*, Yale University Press, New Haven, NJ, and London, 1981.

Ramsay, G., *Sunday Lunch and Other Recipes from the World*, London, Quadrille, 2006.

Randolph, M., *The Virginia Housewife, or Methodical Cook*, Dover Publications, New York, 1993.

Rees, G., 'A Residence in Pall Mall', *L'Intermédiaire des Casanovistes*, année XXIV, 2007, pp. 11–14.

Riello, G., 'A Taste of Italy: Italian Businesses and the Culinary Delicacies in Georgian London', *London Journal*, 2006, vol. 31, no. 2, pp. 201–22.

[Riggs Miller, A.], *Letters from Italy, Describing the Manners, Customs, Antiquities, Paintings, &c. of that Country, in the Years MDCCLXX and MDCCLXXI, to a Friend Residing in France by an English Woman*, 3 vols, Edward and Charles Dilly, London, 1776.

Riley, G., 'Parsnips: Now You See Them – Now You Don't', in *Disappearing Foods: Studies in Foods and Dishes at Risk* (Oxford Symposium on Food and Cookery 1994), ed. Harlan Walker, Prospect, Totnes, 1995, pp. 154–8.

Riley, G., 'Platina, Martino and Their Circle', in *Cooks & Other People* (Oxford Symposium on Food and Cookery 1995), ed. Harlan Walker, Prospect Books, Totnes, 1996, pp. 214–19.

Riley, G., *The Oxford Companion to Italian Food*, Oxford University Press, Oxford, 2007.

Roden, C., *The Food of Italy*, Chatto & Windus, London, 1989.

Ronay, E., *The Unforgettable Dishes of My Life. Recipes.* Sphere Books, London 1991.

Rylance, R., *The Epicure's Almanack. Eating and Drinking in Regency London: the Original 1815 Guidebook*, ed. Janet Ing Freeman, The British Library, London, 2012.

Sacchi, Bartolomeo, *see* Platina.

Sass, H., *A Journey to Rome and Naples, Performed in 1817; Giving an Account of the Present State of Society in Italy; and Containing Observations on the Fine Arts*, Longman, Hurst, Rees, Orme & Brown, London, 1818.

Savonarola, M., *Libreto de tutte le cosse che se magnano; un'opera di dietetica del sec. XV*, ed. Jane Nysted, Almqvist & Wiskell International, Stockholm, 1988.

Scappi, B., *The Opera of Bartolomeo Scappi (1570), L'arte et prudenza d'un maestro cuoco*, translated and with commentary by Terence Scully, University of Toronto Press, Toronto, ONT, and London, 2008.

Scholliers, P., *Food, Drink and Identity: Cooking, Eating and Drinking in Europe since the Middle Ages*, Berg, Oxford, 2001.

Scott Sutherland, A., *The Spaghetti Tree. Mario and Franco and the Trattoria Revolution*, Primavera Books, London, 2009.

Schwartz, A., *Naples at Table: Cooking in Campania*, Harper Collins, New York, NY, 1998.

Scully, T., *The Art of Cookery in the Middle Ages*, Boydell Press, Woodbridge, 1995.

Serventi, S., (ed.), *Il cuoco piemontese perfezionato a Parigi*, Slow Food Editore, Bra, 1995.

Serventi, S., and F. Sabban, *Pasta: the Story of a Universal Food*, Columbia University Press, New York, NY, 2002.

Shepherd, R., *Sherlock Holmes's London*, CICO Books, London, 2015.

Silverman, K., *Lightning Man: the Accursed Life of Samuel F. B. Morse*, Alfred Knopf, New York, 2003.

Sitwell, W., *Eggs or Anarchy*, Simon & Schuster, London, 2016.

Smith, A. F., *The Oxford Companion to American Food*, Oxford University Press, Oxford, 2007.

Smollett, T., *Travels Through France and Italy*, Tauris Parke Paperbacks, London, 2010.

Soyer, A., *The Modern Housewife or Ménagère. Comprising nearly one thousand receipts …*, Simkin Marshall & Co., London, 1849.

Soyer, N., *Soyer's Standard Cookery. A Complete Guide to the Art of Cooking Dainty, Varied and Economical Dishes for the Household*, Andrew Melrose, London, 1912.

Spang, R. L., *The Invention of the Restaurant. Paris and Modern Gastronomic Culture*, Harvard University Press, Cambridge, MA, 2000.

Sparti, D. L., 'Il diario di viaggio (1663–66) di Sir Philip Skippon: arte e società nell'Italia del Seicento', *Bollettino del C.I.R.V.I.*, anno XIX, vol. 37/38, fascs. I/II, 1998, pp. 103–200.

Sponza, L., *Italian Immigrants in Nineteenth-Century Britain: Realities and Images*, Leicester University Press, Leicester, 1988.

Sponza, L., 'Italian "Penny Ice-Men" in Victorian London', in Anne J. Kershen (ed.), *Food in the Migrant Experience*, Ashgate, Aldershot, 2002.

Starke, M., *Letters from Italy*, Thomas Gillet for R. Phillips, London, 1800.

Stead, J., 'Quizzing Glasse: or Hannah Scrutinized', in Hannah Glasse, *'First Catch Your Hare…' The Art of Cookery Made Plain and Easy by a Lady. A Facsimile of the First Edition*, Prospect Books, London, 2012, pp. xv–xxxi.

Stendhal (Henri-Marie Beyle), 'Rome, Naples et Florence (1826) in Victor Del Litto (ed.), *Voyages en Italie*, Gallimard (Bibliothèque de la Pléiade), Paris, 1973.

Stenton, F. M., *Anglo-Saxon England*, Clarendon Press, Oxford, 1971.

Stevens-Cox, J., (ed.), *Ice-creams of Queen Victoria's Reign*, The Toucan Press, Guernsey, 1970.

Story, W. W., *Roba di Roma*, 2 vols, Houghton Mifflin, Boston and New York, 1893.

Stuart, T., *The Bloodless Revolution. A Cultural History of Vegetarianism from 1600 to Modern Times*, W. W. Norton & Company, New York and London, 2008.

Tames, R., *Feeding London. A Taste of History*, Historical Publications, London, 2003.

Taste & Smell in the Eighteenth Century, special issue of *De Achttiende Eeuw*, v. 48, no. 1/2, 2016.

Taruschio, A. and F., *Leaves from the Walnut Tree: Recipes of a Lifetime*, Pavilion Books, London, 1993.

Thick, M., *The Neat House Gardens.* Prospect Books, Totnes, 1998.

Thick, M., *Sir Hugh Plat. The Search for Useful Knowledge in Early Modern London.* Prospect Books, Totnes, 2010.

Thick, M., 'The Contrasting Histories of Florence Fennel, Spanish Cardoons, Broccoli and Celeriac in England from the Early Eighteenth Century Until the 1970s', in *Disappearing Foods: Studies in Foods and Dishes at Risk* (Oxford Symposium on Food and Cookery 1994), ed. Harlan Walker, Prospect Books, Totnes, 1995, pp. 204-14.

Thirsk, J., *Food in Early Modern England*, Continuum, London, 2007.

Thomas, W., *The Historie of Italie*, Thomas Berthelet, London, 1549.

Thomas, W., *Principal Rules of the Italian Grammer: with a Dictionarie for the Better Vunderstandynge of Boccacce, Petrarcha and Dante*, [Thomas Powell], London, 1562.

Tomasi di Lampedusa, G., *Il Gattopardo*, Feltrinelli, Milan, 1958.

Torkington, R., *Ye Oldest Diarie of Englysshe Travell Being the Hitherto Unpublished Narrative of the Pilgrimage of Sir Richard Torkington to Jerusalem in 1517*, ed. William J. Loftie, Fiel & Tuer, London, 1884.

[Trevisan, A.], *A Relation or Rather a True Account of the Island of England; with Sundry Particulars of the Customs of these People, and of the Royal Revenues Under King Henry the Seventh, About the Year 1500*, ed. Charlotte Augusta Sneyd, Camden Society, London, 1847.

Turner, J., *Spice. The History of a Temptation*, Harper Perennial, London, 2005.

Tryon, T., *The Way to Health, Long Life and Happiness*, London, 1683.

Twain, M., *A Tramp Abroad*, Oxford University Press, Oxford and New York, NY, 1996.

Verrall, W., *A Complete System of Cookery*, [Printed for the Author], London, 1759.

Vigilio, G. B., *La insalata. Cronaca mantovana dal 1561 al 1602*, Daniela Ferrari and Cesare Mozzarelli (eds), Mantua, Arcari, 1992.

Walchester, K., *'Our own Fair Italy': Nineteenth-Century Women's Travel Writing and Italy 1800-1844*, Peter Lang, Oxford, 2007.

Warde, A., and L. Martens, *Eating Out. Social Differentiation, Consumption and Pleasure.* Cambridge University Press, Cambridge, 2000.

Warneke, S., *Images of the Educational Traveller in Early Modern England*, Brill, Leiden, 1995.

Waters, A., *Chez Panisse Cookbook*, Harper Books, New York, NY, 1999.

Waters, A., *Coming to my Senses*, Hardie Grant, London, 2017.

Webb, D., *Pilgrims and Pilgrimage in the Medieval West*, I. B. Tauris, London and New York, 1999.

Wilson, C. A., *Food and Drink in Britain*, Penguin Books, Harmondsworth, 1976.

Wilson, T. M., *Food, Drink and Identity in Europe* (European Studies 22), Amsterdam and New York, NY, 2006.

The Works of Geoffrey Chaucer, ed. Fred N. Robinson, Oxford University Press, London, 1957.

Wright, C. A., 'Cucina arabo-sicula and Maccharruni' in *Al-Masāq: studia arabo-islamica mediterranea*, vol. 9, 1996–7, pp. 151–77.

Wright, C. A., 'The History of Macaroni', www.cliffordawright.com/history/macaroni.html.

Yates, F. A., *John Florio. The Life of an Italian in Shakespeare's England*, Cambridge University Press, Cambridge, 1934.

Zancani, D., 'Do We Know What They Really Ate? Interpreting the Names of Medieval Foods in Italy', in Anna Laura Lepschy and Arturo Tosi (eds), *L'italiano a tavola. Linguistic and Literary traditions*, Guerra Edizioni, Perugia, 2010.

Zancani, D., 'The Notion of "Lombard" and "Lombardy" in the Middle Ages', in Alfred P. Smyth (ed.), *Medieval Europeans*, Macmillan, Basingstoke, 1998.

Zellner, W., 'Tom Monaghan: the Fun-Loving Prince of Pizza', in *Business Week*, 8 February 1988, p. 90.

MANUSCRIPTS AND PRINTED EPHEMERA

Oxford, Bodleian Library, John Johnson Collection of Printed Ephemera:

Bill Headings: 12 (9), (85); 13 (4), (19), (52); 19 (66), (68), (69).

Menus: City Companies 2 (11-13), (17).

Menus: Hotels and Restaurants 5 (9 a,c,d), (16b), (32b), (34), (47).

Oxford Trade 5 (30).

Trade Cards: 9 (95); 11 (37a); 12 (42), (45).

Tradesmen's Lists folder

Lennox Boyd Collection: Bill Headings (Scotland)

Manuscripts:

Oxford, Bodleian Library, MS. Don. e. 11.

Oxford, Bodleian Library, MS Eng. Misc. d. 437.

Oxford, Bodleian Library, MS. Eng. Misc. e. 589.

Piacenza, Biblioteca Comunale, MS. Comun. 556.

PICTURE CREDITS

INDEX

To Valentina

First published in 2019 by the Bodleian Library
Broad Street, Oxford OX1 3BG
www.bodleianshop.co.uk

ISBN 978 1 85124 512 3

PUBLISHER'S NOTE
The historical recipes quoted or described
in this book have not been tested.

We are grateful to Prospect Books for their permission to reproduce recipes from *Cooking Apicius: Roman Recipes for Today* by S. Grainger, London, 2006 and *Apicius, a critical edition with an introduction and English Translation* by C. Grocock and S. Grainger, London, 2006.

Cover design by Dot Little at the Bodleian Library
Designed and typeset by Laura Parker in 10 pt on 16 pt RenardNo2
Printed and bound by Printer Trento on 120gsm Tauro Offset paper

British Library Catalogue in Publishing Data
A CIP record of this publication is available from the British Library